MICROECONOMIC ISSUES TODAY

Alternative Approaches

Third Edition

MICROECONOMIC ISSUES TODAY

Alternative Approaches
Third Edition

Robert B. Carson
State University College, Oneonta, New York

St. Martin's Press
New York

This book is dedicated to my mother,
Catherine Postlewaite Carson

Library of Congress Catalog Card Number: 82–60457
Copyright © 1983 by St. Martin's Press, Inc.
All Rights Reserved.
Manufactured in the United States of America.
76543
fedcba
For information, write St. Martin's Press, Inc.,
175 Fifth Avenue, New York, N.Y. 10010

cover design: Claire Nelson

ISBN: 0–312–53174–5

ACKNOWLEDGEMENTS

Fig. 7–2 from *Business Week*, June 30, 1980, p. 61. Reprinted by permission of Business Week and the McGraw-Hill Book Company.

Table 7–1 from Campbell R. McConnell, *Economics: Principles and Problems*. Copyright 1981 and reprinted by permission of the McGraw-Hill Book Company.

Fig. 8–1 from *U.S. News and World Report*, August 16, 1982, p. 33. Copyright and reprinted by permission.

Table 8–1 from Roger A. Herriot and Herman P. Miller "The Taxes We Pay," Conference Board Record, May 1971, p. 40, used by permission of THE CONFERENCE BOARD.

Table 8–3 from Peter G. Peterson "No More Free Lunch for the Middle Class," *New York Times Magazine*, January 17, 1981, p. 41. Reprinted by permission of the New York Times Company.

Preface

Since the first appearance of *Microeconomic Issues Today*, and its companion volume, *Macroeconomic Issues Today*, in 1980, the book has enjoyed widespread acceptance among economics instructors. Naturally I am gratified by this acceptance of my work. In particular, I have been both delighted and stimulated by the correspondence received from dozens of instructors and students who have taken the time to write letters suggesting changes or simply commenting on the book's economic dialogue. To all of you who have made the book a success and who, in using it, have helped encourage a return of debate to the sometimes arid domain of economics, I offer my thanks.

When I sat down to prepare this new edition, I was struck by the fact that much had changed within the American economy and in the thinking of American economists in only a few years. It was obvious that a new edition would require extensive revisions. The sections on agriculture, energy, regulation (and deregulation), and income distribution (Issues 1, 3, 5, and 8) have been virtually rewritten to consider recent economic and ideological shifts. Issue 7, on productivity, a problem that promises to be a major concern for the rest of the 1980s, is entirely new.

New and expanded graphs and tables appear throughout the book. I have also added a series of questions, "Anticipating the Arguments," to each issue. Intended to be considered *before* the arguments are read, they touch on some of the major themes and point out a few landmarks that may help guide the student as a topic is developed.

All these changes are designed to enhance, not alter, the pedagogical approach followed in earlier editions. As before, the book requires no background in the methods of economic analysis and, insofar as possible, it avoids the use of economic jargon in favor of everyday language. This edition of *Microeconomic Issues Today*, like the earlier one, stresses the ideological choices that exist in economic thought and that often cause ordinary citizens to be confused about what economists *do* and what economists *believe*. As ever, it is meant to be a provocative book, more interested in provoking discussion and thought than in presenting "right" solutions to problems. It remains committed to the belief that real economic solutions are only possible in a democratic society when all alternatives are known and considered.

Let me explain why I undertook this project in the first place. All too frequently, students begin their study of economics with the impression that economists are bland and monolithic when discussing important issues confronting the general society. We may as well admit that the profession sometimes exhibits a tendency to blandness in its public utterances, but surely any supposed unanimity toward social-policy questions has vanished. With the rise of a large radical caucus within the discipline, beginning in the late 1960s, and the recent resurgence of variations of laissez-faire ideology, any facade of consensus has clearly been broken down. The application of economic theory to issues of public policy more and more reflects a range of choice from Conservative, to Liberal, to Radical.

For the student struggling with basic theory and analytic tools, as well as for the ordinary citizen overwhelmed by economic data in the newspapers and on the TV evening news, it is hard to avoid confusion over what economists really think about the problems facing the nation. This book begins with the assumption that the answers economists give to policy questions can be usefully compared and analyzed according to the particular biases of their arguments and the probable outcomes of their proposals. In other words, differences in economic logic and interpretation of evidence are not so much a function of skill mastery as they are the expression of strongly held social and political opinions. The book also assumes that economics as a body of knowledge takes on greater meaning and is more readily comprehended when it is viewed in this way.

For each issue, a Conservative, Liberal, and Radical analysis and proposed solution are presented in turn as the valid approach to the problem. On one page, there may be a vigorous and unyielding defense of laissez faire and the market economy; on another, a program for the elimination or modification of the free market. This is not the way economic analysis and theory are usually taught, but it is what the practice of economics is about. In the real world, the citizen and the economist make public policy choices that protect, attack, or modify the market mechanism. We may defend our positions in terms of economic logic, but behind our proofs lies our political and ideological view of the world. This book attempts to examine the relationship between ideological values and the economic theories and policies that are their outcome.

Since the book presents a wide range of views on a number of currently sensitive issues, it should provoke disagreement, controversy, and discussion. In itself, the book does not urge a particular ideological position or a particular variety of economic analysis. The decision to select or reject this or that point of view is left, as it should be, to the reader.

Each chapter is self-contained and may be assigned in any order the instructor chooses. (The Instructor's Manual provides a grid correlating the chapters here with the chapters in leading principles textbooks.) There are relatively few footnotes or direct references to particular economists, although the ideas of many contemporary economists and schools of economic thought will be apparent. The bibliography at the end is offered for anyone wishing to dig a little deeper into an issue or a particular economic perspective or approach.

The decision to minimize the explicit discussion of technical terms and specific economic concepts in the discussion of contemporary policy issues does not mean the author rejects the importance of formal economic analysis. For instructors using *Microeconomic Issues Today* along with a conventional principles of economics text, the Instructor's Manual supplies an outline of the pertinent economic concepts and provides graphical analyses. Even instructors using this book as collateral reading may find the manual quite useful.

The basic outline of this book grew out of discussions with Irving Rockwood and my own earlier experience with two collections of readings in economics. As the work developed, I received further encouragement in very early stages from Tony Dick and Murray Curtin, and at a later, and most critical juncture, from Bertrand Lummus.

The publication of this new edition has incurred its own special debts which deserve acknowledgment. Michael Weber of St. Martin's Press took over the editorial responsibilities for this version and was a steady and encouraging influence in developing a revised and fresh edition. Emily Berleth again served brilliantly as project editor. Professor Carolyn Ahern of Monterey Peninsula College and Professor Paul Haas of Bowling Green State University read the new manuscript and made many useful suggestions. Charlize Fazio and Sheridan Herring were sturdy and dependable typists, always patient with the author's awful longhand. Professors David Ring and William O'Dea of the State University of New York at Oneonta aided in preparing the Instructor's Manual. And, as always, there was the inspiration and encouragement given by my students, questioning and demanding answers to the "great" economic problems of the day regardless of whether the author had the foggiest notion of what the "answer" might be.

Contents

PART 1

INTRODUCTION

Alternative Economic Philosophies

A Survey of Conservative, Liberal, and Radical Critiques

The ideas of economists, both when they are right and when they are wrong, are more powerful than is commonly understood. Indeed, the world is ruled by little else. Practical men, who believe themselves to be quite exempt from any intellectual influences, are usually the slaves of some defunct economist. Madmen in authority, who hear voices in the air, are distilling their frenzy from some academic scribbler of a few years back.

John Maynard Keynes, 1936

The Making and Unmaking of Consensus Economics

Today, disagreement among economists is an accepted fact of life. Daily the newspapers and TV bombard us with widely differing analyses of the causes and cures of the nation's woes as proposed by economists and by the politicians who listen to economists. Even introductory economics textbooks are filled with "dissenting" chapters and "alternative" theories. Meanwhile, for many of us on the blackboard side of the desk, the shrillness of the arguments and the sharpness of the debate in economics is both uncomfortable and unfamiliar.

Only a decade and a half ago, most American economists and non-economists were enjoying a blissful state of "consensus" on economic matters. Despite the somewhat divisive, but to most Americans still distant, rumblings from Vietnam, the domestic economic house seemed to be in good order. At the end of 1968, even though a Republican presidential victory in November had changed parties in the White House, there was remarkably little disagreement about basic matters of economic policy. Today, it is difficult to comprehend how such agreement among economists and political leaders ever existed; but if we go back and look at the situation then, it was not a surprising state of affairs.

The economy, by late 1968, had undergone almost seven consecutive years of economic growth. The real output (Gross National Product) of the nation had increased more than 20 percent over that period. Unemployment, which had been more than seven percent when John F. Kennedy came to office in 1961, was less than four percent. Prices, although showing signs of edging upward at the close of the 1960s (there was serious concern about 1968's "big" 4-percent price increase), had been quite stable. Compared to what we have come to accept recently, they were downright constant.

Nothing is more conducive to agreement than good news; virtually everyone wants to have a hand in it. And in explaining the good news in the 1960s, practically all economists (at least those who had a public forum) and a great many non-economists attributed the big boom to the acceptance of new economic doctrines and policy. The "new economics" emphasized an active role for government in stimulating the economy through tax cuts and government spending. John

Maynard Keynes, the originator of most of these "new" ideas twenty-five years earlier, had moved rapidly from being an unknown apostle of the "dismal science" to becoming a household name. In 1968, *Time* and *Newsweek* celebrated the new economics and Lord Keynes (now dead for twenty-two years) by devoting covers and long feature stories to the English economist and his followers. *Time* even suggested, and probably most economists nodded modestly, that the "new economics" now could protect us from the old problems of unemployment and recession as well as flights into price inflation. Richard Nixon, campaigning hard in 1968 for the presidency, even allowed to reporters that he too was a Keynesian on domestic economic matters. The implication was obvious: *Wasn't everybody?*

Within a few years, the Camelot enjoyed by so many economists was over. It did not end slowly, nor did any single event destroy it; yet, by the mid 1970s, economic consensus was about as easy to find as the much-celebrated missing eighteen minutes on the Nixon tapes. The War in Vietnam had had its effect—dividing men and women of principle in a way the nation had never experienced before. In particular the war created a new breed of young economists who not only questioned the political and economic policies that dragged the nation into Vietnam but who also challenged all the assumptions that underlay a production-for-profit capitalist economy. Meanwhile, as the economy stumbled into recession in 1971 and again in 1975, "true believers" in the "new economics" began to be sorely tested. Some held steadfastly to the economics of the 1960s, arguing that it still worked if given a chance. Others were less certain. By the last half of the 1970s, there was a growing group within the economics profession who now saw much error in the old "new economic" ways. To this group, the older "old economics," with its emphasis upon free markets and little government interference, was more attractive.

For ordinary citizens not schooled in the strange jargon and obscure ways of economists there also was confusion. The economy was quite simply unravelling in the 1970s and early 1980s. As it unravelled, different groups of people were hit with different sets of problems. For some workers it was the threat of unemployment. For others it was inflation. Some were distressed by the bigger slice of income being paid in taxes. Others worried about the cessation of transfer payments from government. For businesspeople there was the problem of the rising costs of government regulation of the environment, the workplace, and the marketplace; for the consumer advocate, there was the problem of pollution and product liability.

Faced with the confusing downward drift of the economy, a troubled citizenry could find little help among an increasingly divided economics profession. Moreover, disagreement among economists is downright unsettling. It came as a rude surprise to the ordinary person who, although paying due professional respect to the economists, still sees the economist as a kind of mechanic. When one's car does not start, the car owner expects (at least hopes) that the diagnosis of mechanical trouble given at one garage is exactly the same as what will be heard at any other. If there is one mechanical problem, there should be one mechanical solution. The moral of this comparison is that economics is more than studying a repair manual and economists are not mechanics.

The Role of Ideology

How is such disagreement possible? Isn't economics a science? Economists' answers to that question vary. A common and reasonable enough response is simply that scientists disagree too. While there is much truth to such an answer, it really begs the question. Plainly, the "dismal science" of economics is not a science like physics. While economists may sometimes talk about the laws of supply and demand as if they were eternal verities like the law of gravity, there is abundant anthropological and historical evidence that many societies have behaved quite contrary to the laws of supply and demand. Outside of science fiction, however, there is no denying the law of gravity.

To be sure, economists employ (or at least they should) the rigor of scientific method and quantitative techniques in collecting data, testing hypotheses, and offering reasonable conclusions and predictions. However, economists deal with different "stuff" from that of their colleagues in the exact sciences. Their data involve human beings and their laboratory is a world of behavior and perception that varies with time and place. On top of this, economists, like all social scientists, are called upon to answer a question not asked of those in the "pure" sciences: "What *ought* to be?" Astronomers, for instance, are not asked what *ought* to be the gravitational relationships of our universe. That would be a nonsense question. Economists, however, cannot evade making some determinations about optimal prices, optimal income distribution, and so forth. Their decisions, while perhaps based upon a genuine effort at neutrality, detachment, and honest evaluation of the available evidence, finally must be a matter of interpretation, a value judgment based upon their own particular world views. To put the point directly: Economics, as a study of human behavior, cannot avoid value judgments. Struggle as it may, economics as a discipline is never free from ideology.

Until the recent period of economic difficulty, economists haven't talked much about ideology, or their individual political views of the world. "Ideology" has been somehow a dirty word, or unprofessional, or it has been too troublesome to deal with. Thus, differences of opinion among economists usually were treated only as "theoretical" disagreements. And of course in the booming sixties there weren't many theoretical disagreements anyway. Those that disagreed with the dominant "new economics" were driven to the margins of influence or simply dismissed as "quacks."

However, as the pressure of the crises within the economy and society heightened in the late 1960s and through the 1970s, the economics profession more and more found itself shifting from debate over merely "theoretical" questions to those centering on concrete political issues. The *Newsweek* editorials of the Conservative Milton Friedman and the Liberal Lester Thurow show that leaders of the profession now fearlessly parade their politics as they offer their particular analyses of economic problems. Meanwhile, the shrill debate between conventional economists and those of a more radical persuasion has forced increased attention to political economic alternatives. For good or ill, the economics profession has become involved in politics and in recommending political courses of action to pursue economic objectives.

The significance of these trends should not be lost on the beginning student of economics. The above arguments hold that the content and application of economic reasoning are determined finally by the force of what people believe, not by an independent and neutral logic. But to say that economics is a matter of opinion is not to say that it is just a study of relatively different ideas: Here's this view and here's that one and each is of equal value. In fact, opinions are not of equal value. There are good opinions and there are bad ones. Economic ideas have different consequences when adopted as policy. They have different effects, now and in the future. As we confront the various policy solutions proposed to deal with the many crises now gnawing deep into our economy and society, we must make choices. This one seems likely to produce desired outcomes. That one does not. No other situation is consistent with a free and reasoned society. Granted it is a painful situation, since choice always raises doubts and uncertainty and runs the risk of wrong judgment, but it cannot be evaded.

This short book is intended to focus on a limited number of the hard choices that we must make. Its basic premise is that economic judgment is basically a matter of learning to choose the best policy solution among all possible solutions. This book further assumes that failure to make this choice is to underestimate the richness and importance of the economic ideas we learn and to be blind to the fact that ideas and analysis do indeed apply to the real world of our own lives.

On Sorting Out Ideologies

Assuming we have been at least partially convincing in our argument that economic analysis is permeated by ideological judgment, we now turn to examine the varieties of ideology common to American economic thought.

In general, we may characterize the ideological position of contemporary economics and economists as Conservative, Liberal, or Radical. These, the same handy categories that evening newscasters use to describe political positions, presumably have some meaning to people. The trouble with labels, though, is that they can mean a great deal and, at the same time, nothing at all. At a distance the various political colors of Conservative, Liberal, and Radical banners are vividly different. Close up, though, the distinctiveness blurs, and what seemed obvious differences are not so clear. For instance, there is probably *not* a strictly Liberal position on every economic issue, nor are all the economists who might be generally termed "Liberal" in consistent agreement. The same is true in the case of many Radical or Conservative positions as well. Unless we maintain a certain open-endedness in our categorizing of positions, the discussion of ideological differences will be overly simple and much too rigid. Therefore, the following generalizations and applications of ideological typologies will attempt to isolate and identify only "representative" positions. By doing this we can at least focus on the differences at the center rather than on the fuzziness at the fringes of schools of thought.

We are still left with a problem. How do you specify an ideological position? Can you define a Radical or a Liberal or a Conservative position? The answer here is simple enough. As the British economist Joan Robinson once observed, an ideology is like an elephant—you can't define an elephant but you should know one when you see it. Moreover, you should know the difference between an elephant and a horse or a cow without having to resort to definitions.

There is a general framework of thought within each of the three ideological schools by which we can recognize them. Thus we will not "define" the schools but merely describe the salient characteristics of each. In all the following, the reader is urged to remember that there are many varieties of elephants. Our specification of a particular ideological view on any issue is a representative model—a kind of average-looking elephant (or horse or cow). Thus, the Conservative view offered on the problem of inflation, for instance, should not be thought of as the only possible expression of Conservative thought on this question. However, it should be sufficiently representative so that the basic Conservative paradigm, or world view, can be distinguished from the Radical or Liberal argument. Where truly important divisions within an ideological paradigm exist, the divisions will be appropriately noted and discussed.

THE CONSERVATIVE PARADIGM

What is usually labeled the Conservative position in economic thought and policy making was not always "Conservative." Conservative ideas may be traced to quite radical origins. The forebears of modern Conservative thought—among them England's Adam Smith (1723–1790)—were not interested in "conserving" the economic order they knew but in destroying it. In 1776, when Smith wrote his classic *Wealth of Nations,* England was organized under a more-or-less closed economic system of monopoly rights, trade restriction, and constant government interference with the marketplace and with an individual's business and private affairs. This system, known as mercantilism, had been dominant in England and, with slight variations, elsewhere on the Continent for over 250 years.

Adam Smith's Legacy   Smith's remedy was simple enough: Remove all restrictions on commercial and industrial activity and allow the market to work freely. The philosophical basis of Smith's argument rested on his beliefs that (1) all men had the natural right to obtain and protect their property; (2) all men were by nature materialistic; and (3) all men were rational and would seek, by their own reason, to maximize their material well-being. These individualistic tendencies in men would be tempered by competition in the marketplace. There men would have to compromise with one another to gain any individual satisfaction whatsoever. The overall effect of these compromises ultimately would lead to national as well as individual satisfaction. Competition and self-interest would keep prices down and production high and rising. They also would stimulate product improvement, invention, and steady economic progress. For this to happen, of course, there would have to be a minimum of interference with the free market—no big government, no powerful unions, and no conspiring in trade. Smith's position and that of his contemporaries and followers was known as "Classical Liberalism." The Conservative label now applied to these views seems to have been affixed much later, when Smith's heirs found themselves acting in the defense of a status quo rather than opposing an older order.

Thus, modern capitalist economic thought must trace its origins to Adam Smith. While this body of thought has been built upon and modified over the past 200 years, the hand of Adam Smith is evident in every conventional economics textbook. Common sense tells us, however, that a lot has changed since Smith. Today business is big. There are labor unions and big government to interfere with his balanced free market of equals. His optimistic view of a naturally growing and expanding system is now replaced by growth problems and by a steady dose of pessimism in most glances toward the future. Nevertheless, modern Conservatives, among contemporary defenders of capitalism, still stand close to the ideals of Adam Smith.

Modern Conservative thought is anchored to two basic philosophic ideas that distinguish it from Liberal and Radical positions. First, the market system and the spirit of competition are central to proper social organization. Second, individual rights and freedoms must be unlimited and uninfringed.

Conservatives oppose any "unnatural" interference in the marketplace. In particular, the Conservative views the growth of big government in capitalist society as the greatest threat to economic progress. Milton Friedman, Nobel Laureate and preeminent figure in the Conservative Chicago school, has argued that government has moved from being merely an instrumentality necessary to sustain the economic and social order and become an instrument of oppression. Friedman's prescription for what "ought to be" on the matter of government is clear:

> A government which maintained law and order, defined property rights, served as a means whereby we could modify property rights and other rules of the economic game, adjudicated disputes about the interpretation of the rules, enforced contracts, promoted competition, provided a monetary framework, engaged in activities to counter technical monopolies and to overcome neighborhood effects widely regarded as sufficiently important to justify government intervention, and which supplemented private charity and the private family in protecting the irresponsible, whether madman or child—such a government would clearly have important functions to perform. The consistent liberal is not an anarchist.*

The antigovernment position of Conservatives in fact goes further than merely pointing out the dangers to individual freedom. To Conservatives, the growth of big government itself causes or worsens economic problems. For instance, the growth of elaborate government policies to improve the conditions of labor, such as minimum-wage laws, social security protection, and the like, are seen as actually harming labor in general. A wage higher than that determined by the market will provide greater income for some workers, but, the Conservative argument runs, it will reduce the total demand for labor and thus dump many workers into unemployment. As this example indicates, the Conservative assault on big government is seen not simply as a moral or ethical question but also in terms of alleged economic effects.

Another unifying feature of the representative Conservative argument is its emphasis on individualism and individual freedom. To be sure, there are those in the Conservative tradition who pay only lip service to this view, but for true Conservatives it is the centerpiece of their logic. As Friedman has expressed it:

> We take freedom of the individual . . . as the ultimate goal in judging social arguments. . . . In a society freedom has nothing to say about what an individual does with his freedom; it is not an all-embracing ethic. Indeed, the major aim of the liberal [here meaning conservative as we use

*Milton Friedman, *Capitalism and Freedom* (Chicago: University of Chicago Press, 1962), p. 34.

the term] is to leave the ethical problem for the individual to wrestle with.*

Modern Conservatives as a group exhibit a wide variety of special biases. Not all are as articulate or logically consistent as Friedman's Chicago school. Many are identified more readily by what they oppose than what they seem to be for. While big government, in both its microeconomic interferences and its macroeconomic policy making, is the most obvious common enemy, virtually any institutionalized interference with individual choice is at least ceremonially opposed.

Some critics of the Conservative position are quick to point out that most modern-day Conservatives are not quite consistent on the question of individual freedom when they focus on big business. In fact, until comparatively recently, Conservatives usually did demand the end of business monopoly. Like all concentrations of power, it was viewed as an infringement upon individual rights. The Austrian economist Joseph Schumpeter argued that "Big Business is a half-way house on the road to Socialism." The American Conservative Henry C. Simons observed in the depressed 1930s that "the great enemy to democracy is monopoly." Accounting for the change to a more accommodating position on big business is not easy. Conservatives seem to offer two basic reasons. First, big business and the so-called monopoly problem have been watched for a long period of time, and the threat of their power subverting freedom is seen as vastly overstated. Second, by far the larger problem is the rise of big government, which is cited as the greatest cause of business inefficiency and monopoly misuse. Another factor that seems implied in Conservative writing is the fear of communism and socialism, both internal and external. To direct an assault on the American business system, even if existing business concentration were a slight impediment to freedom, would lay that system open to direct Radical attack. How serious this supposed contradiction in Conservative logic really is remains a matter of debate among its critics.

The Recent Resurgence of Conservative Economic Ideas In the United States, until the drab years of the Great Depression, what we now call "Conservative economics" *was* economics, period. Except for an occasional voice challenging the dominant wisdom, usually to little

*Ibid., p. 12.

effect, there were few among economists, political leaders, or members of the public at large who disagreed greatly with Adam Smith's emphasis on individual freedom and on a free-market economic condition.

The Depression years, however, brought a strong reaction to this kind of political and economic thinking. Many—perhaps most—of the millions of Americans who were out of work in the 1930s and the millions more who hung on to their jobs by their teeth came to believe that a "free" economy was simply one in "free fall." While most staunch Conservatives complained bitterly about the abandoning of market economics and about the "creeping socialism" of Franklin Roosevelt's New Deal, they had few listeners. For thirty-two of the next forty-eight years after FDR's election in 1932, the White House, and usually the Congress, was in "liberal" Democratic hands. For Conservatives, however, perhaps the greater losses were in the universities, where the old free-market "truths" of Adam Smith and his disciples quickly fell out of style. In their place, a generation of professors espoused the virtues of the "new economics" of John Maynard Keynes and the view that a capitalist economy "requires" government intervention to keep it from destroying itself.

Driven to the margins of academic and political influence by the 1970s, the Conservatives seemed in danger of joining the dinosaur and dodo bird as an extinct species. But as the old Bob Dylan song goes, "the times, they are a-changing." By the late 1970s, in the aftermath of Vietnam and the Watergate scandal and in a period when nothing government did seemed able to control domestic inflation and unemployment problems, there developed a growing popular reaction against government in general. As more and more Americans came to believe that government economic and social interventions were the cause of the nation's maladies, the Conservative ideology took off again under its own power.

In 1980, the Conservative economic and political paradigm succeeded in recapturing the White House. Ronald Reagan became the first president since Herbert Hoover to come to office after a private-sector career. There was no doubting Reagan's philosophical commitment to the principles of a free-enterprise economy.

As might be expected, Conservatives found themselves facing a difficult situation. Implementing a free-market policy was of course much easier to accomplish in argument than in the real world—especially in a world vastly more complex than that envisioned by Adam Smith. "Reaganomics," the popular catchword for the new brand of Conservative economics, was quickly and sorely tested as the economy slipped into a deep recession in late 1981. To both friendly and hostile critics, Conservatives responded that quick solutions were not possible since the economic debris of a half-century needed to be swept aside before the economy could be reconstructed. Whether or not the Conservative broom ultimately will prove sufficient for the task remains to be seen, but economic ideas that have been shunned in serious political and economic debates for over forty years are back in style.

THE LIBERAL PARADIGM

According to a national opinion poll, Americans tend to associate the word "Liberal" with big government, Franklin Roosevelt, labor unions, and welfare. Time was, not too long ago, when "Liberal" stood not just as a proud appellation but seemed fairly to characterize the natural drift of the whole country. At the height of his popularity and before the Vietnam war toppled his administration, Lyndon Johnson, speaking of the new "Liberal" consensus, observed:

> After years of ideological controversy, we have grown used to the new relationship between government, households, business, labor and agriculture. The tired slogans that made constructive discourse difficult have lost their meaning for most Americans. It has become abundantly clear that our society wants neither to turn backward the clock of history nor to discuss the present problems in a doctrinaire or partisan spirit.

Although what we will identify as the "Liberal" position in American economic thought still dominates the teaching and practice of economic reasoning (as we shall see, even some Conservatives have adopted elements of the Liberal analysis), the Liberal argument is undergoing considerable changes. The changes, however, are more cosmetic than basic, and the central contours of Liberal belief are still visible.

The "Interventionist" Faith   While Conservatives and Radicals are comparatively easily identified by a representative position, Liberals are more difficult. In terms of public policy positions, the Liberal spectrum ranges all the way from those favoring a very moderate level of government intervention to those advocating broad government planning of the economy.

Despite the great distance between the defining poles of Liberal thought, several basic points can be stated as unique to the Liberal paradigm. First, like their Conservative counterparts, Liberals are defenders of the principle of private property and the business system. These, however, are not categorical rights, as we observed in the Conservative case. Individual claims to property or the ability to act freely in the marketplace are subject to the second Liberal principle—that social welfare and the maintenance of the entire economy supersede individual interest. In a vicious condemnation of what we would presently call the Conservative position, John Maynard Keynes directly assaulted the philosophical grounds that set the individual over society. Keynes argued:

> It is not true that individuals possess a prescriptive "natural liberty" in their economic activities. There is no "compact" conferring perpetual rights on those who Have or on those who Acquire. The world is not so governed from above that private and social interest always coincide. It is not a correct deduction from the Principles of Economics that enlightened self-interest always operates in the public interest. Nor is it true that self-interest generally is enlightened; more often individuals acting separately to promote their own ends are too ignorant or too weak to attain even these. Experience does not show that individuals, when they make up a social unit, are always less clear-sighted than when they act separately.*

To the Liberal, then, government intervention in, and occasional direct regulation of, aspects of the national economy is neither a violation of principle nor an abridgement of "natural economic law." The benefits to the whole society from intervention simply outweigh any natural right claims. The forms of intervention may vary but their pragmatic purpose is obvious—to tinker and manipulate in order to produce greater social benefits.

Government intervention and regulation go back several decades in American history. The Progressives of the early twentieth century were the first to support direct government regulation of the economy. Faced with the individual and collective excesses of the giant en-

---

*John M. Keynes, "The End of Laissez Faire," in *Essays in Persuasion* (New York: Norton, 1963), p. 68.

terprises of the era of the Robber Barons, the Progressives followed a number of reformist paths in the period from 1900 to 1920. One was the regulation of monopolistic enterprise, to be accomplished either through direct antitrust regulation or by stimulating competition. Pursuit of these policies was entrusted to a new government regulatory agency, the Federal Trade Commission (created in 1914), an expanded Justice Department and court system, and greater state regulatory powers. Second, indirect business regulation was effected by such Progressive developments as legalization of unions, the passage of social legislation at both the federal and state levels, tax reforms, and controls over production (for example, laws against food adulteration)—all of which tended to circumvent the power of business and subject it to the public interest.

Although the legislation and leadership of the administrations of Theodore Roosevelt, William Howard Taft, and Woodrow Wilson went a long way in moderating the old laissez-faire ideology of the previous era, actual interference in business affairs remained slight until the Great Depression. By 1933 perhaps as many as one out of every three Americans was out of work (the official figures said 25 percent), business failures were common, and the specter of total financial and production collapse hung heavy over the whole country. In the bread lines and shantytowns known as "Hoovervilles" as well as on Main Street, there were serious mutterings that the American business system had failed. Business leaders, who had always enjoyed a hero status in the history books and even among ordinary citizens, had become pariahs. Enter at this point Franklin Roosevelt, the New Deal, and the modern formulation of "Liberal" government-business policies. Despite violent attacks upon him from the Conservative media, FDR pragmatically abandoned his own conservative roots and, in a bewildering series of legislative enactments and presidential decrees, laid the foundation of "public interest" criteria for government regulation of the marketplace. *Whatever might work was tried.* The National Recovery Administration (NRA) encouraged industry cartels and price setting. The Tennessee Valley Authority (TVA) was an attempt at publicly owned enterprise. At the Justice Department, Attorney General Thurman Arnold initiated more antitrust actions than all of his predecessors. And a mass of "alphabet agencies" was created to deal with this or that aspect of the Depression.

Intervention to protect labor and extensions of social welfare provisions were not enough to end the Depression. It was the massive spending for World War II that finally restored prosperity. With this prosperity came the steady influence of Keynes, who had argued in the 1930s that only through government fiscal and monetary efforts to keep up the demand for goods and services could prosperity be reached and maintained. Keynes's arguments for government policies to maintain high levels of investment and hence employment and consumer demand became Liberal dogma. To be a Liberal was to be a Keynesian and vice versa.

Alvin Hansen, Keynes's first and one of his foremost proponents in the United States, could scarcely hide his glee in 1957 as he described the Liberal wedding of Keynesian policies with the older government interventionist position this way:

> Within the last few decades the role of the economist has profoundly changed. And why? The reason is that economics has become operational. It has become operational because we have at long last developed a mixed public–private economy. This society is committed to the welfare state and full employment. The government is firmly in the driver's seat. In such a world, practical policy problems became grist for the mill of economic analysis. Keynes, more than any other economist of our time, has helped to rescue economics from the negative position to which it had fallen to become once again a science of the Wealth of Nations and the art of Political Economy.*

Despite the Liberal propensity for tinkering—either through selected market intervention or through macro policy action—most Liberals, like Conservatives, still rely upon supply-and-demand analysis to explain prices and market performance. Their differences with Conservatives on the functioning of markets, determination of output, pricing, and so forth lie not so much in describing what is happening as in evaluating how to respond to what is happening. For instance, there is little theoretical difference between Conservatives and Liberals on how prices are determined under monopolistic conditions. However, to the Conservative, the market itself is the best regulator and

---

*Alvin H. Hansen, *The American Economy* (New York: McGraw-Hill, 1957), p. 175.

preventive of monopoly abuse. To the Liberal, monopoly demands government intervention.

Varieties of Liberal Belief   As noted before, the Liberal dogma covers a wide spectrum of opinion. Moreover, the Liberal position has shifted somewhat in response to the past decade's economic disappointments. On the extreme "left wing" of the Liberal spectrum, economists such as Robert Heilbroner and John Kenneth Galbraith have argued that capitalism as a system described and analyzed in conventional economic theory simply does not exist any longer. To this group, it is no longer important even to pretend capitalism works.

Robert Heilbroner points to the crisis within capitalism as basic to capitalism itself. He argues: "The persistent breakdowns of the capitalist economy, whatever their immediate precipitating factors, can all be traced to a single underlying cause. This is the anarchic or planless character of capitalist production."* This planlessness, according to Heilbroner, sets the stage for government to act as a necessary regulator.

To the left-leaning and always iconoclastic John Kenneth Galbraith, who sees problems of technology rather than profit dominating the giant corporation, a more rational atmosphere for decision making must be created. In brief, the modern firm demands a high order of internal and external planning of output, prices, and capital. The interests of the firm and state become fused in this planning process, and the expanded role of Liberal government in the whole economy and society becomes obvious. While Galbraith currently maintains that he is a socialist, the Liberal outcome of his program is obvious in that (1) he never explicitly takes up the expropriation of private property, and (2) he still accepts a precarious social balance between public and private interest.

While Galbraith's Liberalism leads to the planned economy, most Liberals stop well before this point. Having rejected the logic of self-regulating markets and accepted the realities of giant business enterprise, Liberals unashamedly admit to being pragmatic tinkerers—ever adjusting and interfering with business decision making in an effort to assert the changing "public interest." Yet all this must be done while still respecting basic property rights and due process. Under these ar-

---

*Robert Heilbroner, *The Limits of American Capitalism* (New York: Harper & Row, 1966), p. 88.

rangements business regulation amounts to a protection of business it-self as well as the equal protection of other interest groups in pluralist American society.

In the not-too-distant past, business itself adapted to and em-braced this position. While certain government actions might be op-posed, the philosophy of government intervention in the economy was not necessarily seen as antibusiness. The frequent Conservative depiction of most Liberals as being opposed to the business system does not withstand the empirical test. For instance, in 1964 Henry Ford II organized a highly successful businessmen's committee for Lib-eral Lyndon Johnson while Conservative Barry Goldwater, with Friedman as his advisor, gained little or no big-business support. However, the extent of government regulation soon reached a level that was wholly unacceptable to the private sector. In the late 1960s and early 1970s a blizzard of environmental, job-safety, consumer-protection, and energy regulations blew out of Washington. Added to what was already on the ground, the new legislative snowfall seemed to many businessmen at the end of the 1970s about to bring American business to a standstill. Many who a decade before frankly feared the economic "freedom" of the Conservative vision now embraced that position.

After nearly a decade of economic distress and in the wake of a growing popular sentiment against government authority as expressed through the Reagan victory, most Liberal "interventionists" are frankly confused. Many can be counted upon to hold onto their old commitment to pragmatic tinkering, especially those whose interests are closely and narrowly tied to special-interest groups—environmen-talists, consumer advocates, the poor, minorities, labor unions, and so forth. Others are beginning to rethink their position on interven-tionism. To this group, it is not a question of abandoning the basic concept of government intervention in the economy—that would be an admission that the Conservatives' view of self-balancing economy was essentially correct. Rather, the problem is to redefine what kind of intervention is desirable.

More and more, Liberals admit the failure of past interventionist programs: social assistance, the use of regulatory agencies, corporate and personal income tax policies, and many more of the centerpieces of Liberal economic legislation. Many have backed off from their ear-lier tendency to slap a government bandaid onto any and every economic problem.* Others argue simply that the problem is only to find better solutions, not to stop undertaking the problems.

The present-day ambivalence of Liberals on the degree and type of intervention will be evident in our survey of economic issues in this book; nevertheless, this tendency should not be misunderstood. Specific Liberal approaches to problem solving may be debatable, but the essence of Liberal economics remains unchanged: The capitalist economy simply requires pragmatic adjustment to maintain overall balance and to protect particular elements in the society.

THE RADICAL PARADIGM

Specifying a Radical position would have been no problem a couple of decades ago. Outside of a handful of Marxist scholars, some socialists left over from the 1920s and 1930s, and a few unconventional muckrakers, there was no functioning Radical tradition in American economic thought. However, the two-sided struggles of the 1960s over racism and poverty at home and the war in Vietnam produced a resurgence of Radical critiques. By the mid 1970s, the Radical caucus within the American Economic Association had forced on that body topics for discussion at annual meetings that directly challenged conventional economic thought. The Union of Radical Political Economics (URPE) could boast over 2,000 members and its own journal. Meanwhile, basic textbooks in economics began to add chapters on "Radical economics."

---

*In his *Zero Sum Society*, Lester Thurow, a professor at MIT and a writer for *Newsweek*, has attempted to clarify the modern Liberal's dilemma. According to Thurow, most of our past tinkering has rested on two assumptions: (1) economic growth was not only possible but virtually unavoidable and (2) government could therefore improve the lot of certain groups in the society without seriously damaging the well-being of others. Thurow then proclaims that the falsity of these assumptions is now obvious. With the economic pie not growing in size, a larger slice for one group means a smaller slice for another. For instance, environmental and consumer gains came at the cost of business profits. Business price increases to offset these costs simply redistribute the environmental burden back over the population. While this may seem fair enough, Thurow points out that the economy is a vast collection of many interest groups, each seeking to use government in one way or another to protect itself. Thurow, however, does not throw his hands up in despair. The Liberal solution, he contends, lies in recognizing that all problems are basically distributional problems (who gets what size slice) and therefore in developing a comprehensive economic policy that provides for a rational distribution of income. He does not, however, supply the program.

The Marxist Heritage   Radical economics had arrived—but what, precisely was it? To many nonRadicals it was simply Marxist economics warmed over, but this explanation, though basically true, is too simple. To be sure, the influence of Marx, the leading critic of capitalism, is pervasive in most Radical critiques. But Radical economics is more than Marx. His analysis of capitalism is over one hundred years old and deals with a very different set of capitalist problems. (In Marx's time, capitalism was only in the beginning stages of industrial development and was still characterized by small entrepreneurs carrying on essentially merchant capitalist undertakings.) With this qualification in mind, we will argue, however, that no study of current Radical thought is possible unless one starts with, or at least touches upon, the ideas of Karl Marx. Although a few iconoclastic Radicals will reject a close association with Marxism, the evidence is overwhelming that Marxist analysis is central to understanding the representative Radical position in America today.

Since the Marxist critique is likely to be less familiar to many readers than the basic arguments of Conservatives or Liberals, it is necessary to be somewhat more detailed in specifying the Radical position. As will be quickly apparent, the Radical world view rests on greatly different assumptions about the economic order than those of the Conservatives and the Liberals.

In brief, Marx's scenario for capitalist progress was the following: Depending as they do on the steady accumulation of profit to expand capital and output, capitalists will appropriate surplus labor value from the worker. To capitalists this is a normal and necessary course. If workers were paid, or in any way received, the full value of their labor, capital accumulation, and thus economic growth, would be impossible. However, as this accumulation proceeds, with the steady transference of living labor into capital (what Marx called "dead labor"), capitalists face a crisis. With more and more of their costs reflecting dependence upon capital and with surplus labor value their only source of profits, capitalists are confronted with the reality of not being able to expand surplus. Unless they can exploit labor further by intensifying work, lowering real wages, lengthening the working day, or making similar changes, they face a falling rate of profit on their capital investment. Moreover, with markets limited and workers' ability to consume being constantly reduced, there is a tendency among capitalists to overproduce.

These trends set certain systemic tendencies in motion. Out of the chaos of capitalist competitive struggles for profits in a limited market, there develops a drive toward "concentration and centralization." In other words, the size of businesses grows and the number of enterprises shrinks. However, the problems of the falling rate of profit and chronic overproduction create violent fluctuations in the business cycle. Each depression points ever more clearly toward capitalist economic collapse. Meanwhile, among the increasingly impoverished workers, there is a steady growth of a "reserve army of unemployed"—workers who are now unemployable as production decreases. Simultaneously, increasing misery generates class consciousness and revolutionary activity among the working class. As the economic disintegration of capitalist institutions worsens, the subjective consciousness of workers grows to the point where they successfully overthrow the capitalist system. In the new society the workers themselves take control of the production process, and accumulation for the interest of a narrow capitalist class ceases.

Marx, of course, recognized that these developments would not be perfectly lineal. Capitalists could and would undertake counteracting policies. Greater exploitation, profitable foreign trade, and technological advances could head off temporarily the tendency for profits to fall. Lenin was to add later that imperialism, which amounted to exporting the surplus production problem to underdeveloped nations, also could buy time.

More recently, Paul Baran and Paul Sweezy have argued that the development of monopoly capitalism (along with the imperialist thrust) has allowed the system a respite from the accumulation-and-profit crisis. According to this neo-Marxist interpretation, modern capitalism is monopoly capitalism.* The key institution in the accumulation process remains the business firm, but unlike its predecessors, the modern giant enterprise is an effective "price maker," able to set prices through collective actions so as to maximize total income. However, ending capitalism's tendency toward falling prices is only half the problem. Enough goods still must be sold for a firm to realize income beyond its production costs. In other words, the surplus must rise *and* it must be absorbed. In Keynesian terms, it would be said that

*See Paul Baran and Paul Sweezy, *Monopoly Capital* (New York: Monthly Review Press, 1966). This "revising" of orthodox Marxist theory of capitalist developments is, in one form or another, accepted by most modern Radicals.

effective demand must remain high. According to Baran and Sweezy, monopoly capital has been able to accomplish this in the following ways: (1) by highly effective manipulation of consumer tastes for functionally useless and irrational goods ("the sales effort"), (2) by encouraging a high and increasing government expenditure in both the civilian and military sectors, and (3) by the imperialist domination of overseas markets and sources of raw materials. In all this activity, government is seen as an agent for monopoly capital, shaping its social, fiscal, and foreign policies in order to legitimize the monopoly order and enhance monopoly profits.

While the old capitalist crisis of falling surplus value has been replaced by a tendency for the surplus to rise, most Radicals see this as a temporary development. The old contradictions between capital and labor remain, state actions to maintain demand and to uphold order are not without limits, and the internal crisis of the capitalist economy has exploded into a world struggle among nations. Despite its recent history of success, monopoly capitalism, say the Radicals, will not halt the overall suicidal trajectory of capitalist development. Only the forms and the timing of crisis have changed.

To followers of the Baran and Sweezy critique, probably the most significant of these changes is the alteration of Marx's predictions of proletarian revolution. Revolutionary pressures, rather than rising first from the traditional class of industrial workers, are now greater at the periphery of capitalism—among the exploited populations of Third World nations and the growing subproletariat at home. Monopoly capital may have slowed the growth of exploitation for some workers, but it has greatly increased it for others. Class struggle still looms as the eventual vehicle for capitalism's destruction—but not precisely as Marx had argued.

Marxist analysis is, of course, more penetrating than this short resumé can indicate. One further point that should be examined briefly is Marx's view of the relationship between a society's organization for production and its social relations. To Marx, capitalism was more than economics. Private values, religion, the family, the educational system, and political structures were all shaped by capitalist class domination and by the goal of production for private profit. It is important to recognize this tenet in any discussion of how Marxists—or Radicals with a Marxist orientation—approach contemporary social and economic problems. Marxists do not separate economics from politics or private belief. For instance, racism cannot be abstracted to the level of an ethical question. Its roots are seen in the capitalist production process. Nor is the state ever viewed as a neutrality able to act without class bias. Bourgeois democracy as we know it is seen simply as a mask for class domination. The state is quite simply the tool of dominant interests. To the Marxist, the problem with the system *is* the system; no resolution of capitalist crises is really possible short of changing the system itself.

Marx, in his early writings before his great work, *Capital*, had emphasized the "qualitative" exploitation of capitalism. Modern Radicals have revitalized this early Marx in their "quality-of-life" assaults on the present order. In these they emphasize the problems of worker alienation, commodity fetishism, and the wasteful and useless production of modern capitalism. The human or social problems of modern life are seen as rooted in the way the whole society is geared to produce more and more.

In addition to their Marxist heritage, modern Radicals derive much of their impulse from what they see as the apparent failure of Liberalism. Liberal promises to pursue policies of general social improvement are perceived as actions to protect only *some* interest groups. In general, those benefiting under Liberal arrangements are seen as those who have always gained. The corporation is not controlled. It is more powerful than ever. Rule by elites has not ended nor have the elites changed. Moreover, the national goals of the Liberal ethic—to improve our overall national well-being—have stimulated the exploitation of poor nations, continued the cold war, and increased the militarization of the economy.

The Question of Relevance Quite obviously the Marxist prediction of capitalism's final collapse has not yet come to pass. For critics of the Radical position, this fact, along with certain internal analytic problems, is quite sufficient to consign their critique to the garbage heap. Such a view is somewhat unenlightened. First of all, Marx's ideas in one form or another are more prominent in the world today than the other two ideologies discussed here. Second, Marxism—at least as American Radical scholars have developed and used it—is more a way of looking at the world than a prophecy of things to come. It is the technique of analysis rather than the century-old "truth" of Marx's specific analysis that counts.

As noted before, not all Radicals subscribe to all Marxist doctrine, but Marx in one form or another remains the central element of the Radical challenge. His fundamental contention that the system of private production must be changed remains the badge of membership in the Radical ranks. This sets them apart from mainstream Conservative and Liberal economists.

Critics of Radicalism usually point out that Radical analyses are hopelessly negativistic. Radicals, they say, describe the problems of capitalism without offering a solution other than the end of the whole system. While there is some truth to this charge, we shall see in the following sections that indeed some solutions are offered. But even if their program were vague, Radicals would argue that their greatest contribution is in revealing the truth of the capitalist system.

Somewhat like the Liberals, Radical theorists have been victimized by real-world events. The economic crunch of the 1970s and the recent heating up of the cold war between the USSR and the USA propelled Americans toward Conservative economic values rather than toward the left. Moreover, the old radical constituencies either disappeared, as in the case of the antiwar youth of the 1960s and 1970s, or have been eroded, as in the case of environmental and consumer advocacy. Nevertheless, the force of an idea is not dependent upon the number of true believers. Were that the case, Conservative economic doctrine would have disappeared fifteen years ago. Despite lessened political influence, modern Radical economic thought still looms as a logically important alternative to the more broadly supported Conservative and Liberal paradigms.

Applying the Analysis to the Issues

We have identified representative paradigms; now we will put them to use. The following selected issues by no means exhaust the economic and political crises troubling the nation; nevertheless, this book still should provide a good-sized sampling of the social agenda confronting us. The issues presented here were selected because of their immediacy and representativeness in illustrating the diverse ideological approaches of Conservative, Liberal, and Radical economic analyses.

In each of the following issues, the representative paradigms are presented in a first-person advocacy approach. The reader might do well to regard the arguments like those in a debate. As in a debate, one should be careful to distinguish between substantive differences and mere logical or debating strategies. Thus, some points may be quite

convincing while others seem shallow. However, the reader should remember that, shallow or profound, these are representative political
economic arguments advanced by various economic schools.

The sequence in presenting the paradigms is consistent throughout the text: first Conservative, then Liberal, and finally Radical. In
terms of the logical and historical development of contemporary economic ideologies, this sequence is most sensible; however, it is certainly not necessary to read the arguments in this order. Each one
stands by itself. Nor is any ideological position intentionally set out as
a straw man in any debate.

Readers should look at each position critically. They should test
their own familiarity with economic concepts and their common sense
against what they read in any representative case. Finally, of course,
as students of economics and as citizens, they must make their own
decisions. They determine who, if anyone, is the winner of the debate.

Because of space limitations, the representative arguments are
brief, and some important ideas have been boiled down to a very few
sentences. Also, within each of the three major positions there is a
wide variety of arguments, which may sometimes be at variance with
one another. Conservatives, Liberals, and Radicals disagree among
themselves on specific analyses and programs. For the sake of simplic-
ity, we have chosen not to emphasize these differences but arbitrarily
(although after much thought) have tried to select the most representative arguments. Each paradigm's discussion of an issue presents a critique of present public policy and, usually, a specific program proposal.

In all of the arguments, the factual and empirical evidence offered
has been checked for accuracy. It is instructive in itself that, given the
nature of economic "facts," they can be marshaled to "prove" a great
variety of different ideological positions. Different or even similar evidence supports different truths, depending on the truth we wish to
prove.

PART 2

PROBLEMS IN THE MARKETPLACE

Part 2 focuses upon issues generally accepted by economists as *microeconomic* in their analysis. Microeconomics examines specific economic units—households, firms, industries, labor groups—and how these individual units behave.

The focal point of formal microeconomic analysis since its nineteenth-century origins has been the market. Accordingly, the organization of Part 2 is to look at selected problems in the marketplace. The topics include problems of agricultural supply and demand, consumer market behavior, energy–pricing tradeoffs, firm size, government regulation, productivity, labor unions, and income distribution. Each topic presents some important dimension of market performance; each has been selected for its representative qualities in developing a broadened understanding of microeconomic problems within the contemporary American economy.

American Agriculture
Which Route: Competition or Protection?

Farmers should raise less corn and more Hell.
Mary E. Lease, Kansas, 1890s

Farmers are motivated by just old-fashioned greed.
Robert Berland, Secretary of Agriculture, 1979

I was out in the countryside last week. . . . They're talking
about a full-blown depression. . . . The snowball effect in our
communities is devastating.
Farm Union Organizer, 1982

You can't farm $1500-an-acre land. It'll take all you can produce
to pay the interest.
Bandy Jacobs, Nebraska farmer, 1982

We produce too much food in this country.
Marty Strange, Farmer Advocacy Group, 1982

THE PROBLEM

To many oldtimers, the situation in American farming regions by late 1982 seemed like a page torn out of a history book. Everywhere there were increasing reminders of the Great Depression: rising bank foreclosures of delinquent mortgages, a steady decline in the price of farmland, increased numbers of auctions of farms and farm equipment by farmers who were abandoning their livelihood, and, everywhere, the feeling that hard times would not soon leave. The root of the crisis was not difficult to discover. As Figure 1.1 shows, net farm income had been more or less steadily declining for almost a decade. In fact, by 1982, farm income (in real dollars) was about the same as farmers' net earnings in the mid-1930s.

Only a decade had passed since the first of the big Russian grain deals that had brought farm prices and farm income to all-time highs. Yet somehow the boom times of the mid-1970s seemed light years away. To close observers of American agriculture, however, both boom and bust were common features on the economic landscape. Together they were understood as "the farm problem."

In this century, the rhythm of farm fortune and misfortune had gone like this: first World War I created an exceptional demand for American farm products to feed soldiers and starving civilians. With rising prices resulting, farmers increased their output, but, in the '20s and '30s, after production increased, foreign demand for American farm products declined and prices plummeted. World War II pumped up demand and farm prices; but peace again brought tumbling prices. The several Russian grain deals of the 1970s returned good times, but, squeezed by falling demand and rising output, as well as inflation-fired prices for land, farm equipment, fertilizer, and fuel, farm earnings fell again in the late 1970s.

The farmers took their problems to Washington in the spring of 1979, thundering about the streets in their Harvester and John Deere tractors adorned with placards demanding government aid and higher farm prices. However, they attracted less attention and persuaded fewer politicians than they had hoped. For one thing, the entire country was caught in a troublesome period of inflation. Most Americans felt that the higher prices farmers wanted for their goods would show up at the grocery checkout counter. For another, it was difficult for many citizens to associate economic need with farmers rolling over Washington streets in their huge, $75,000 tractors.

As prices fell and costs rose through 1980, 1981, and 1982, however, there was little denying or ignoring the reappearance of the old farm problem. During past bad times—the 30s, 50s, and 60s, for instance—government had responded with a variety of programs, some purely of an emergency nature and others that were built into the economic structure of American agriculture. These efforts included tariffs on imported farm products, marketing boards, subsidy payments, output quotas, payments for letting land lie idle, and much more. Whether or not these interventions had actually relieved farm distress or only served to worsen the chronic farm problem had long been a matter of debate among economists of different ideological persuasions. That debate had cooled a bit after the Russian grain deals, when farm prices were up and government intervention at a minimum, but the new agricultural crisis of the early 1980s reopened all the old arguments.

The debate over agricultural policy remains an important issue and a profoundly significant theoretical question, since it goes to the very foundation of American economic belief; namely, do free and competitive markets work or do they need constant repair and support by means of government intervention? Exactly how divided economists are on this

FIGURE 1.1   REAL FARM INCOME, 1973–1982

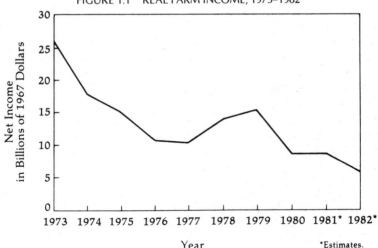

Year   *Estimates.

Source: U.S. Department of Agriculture, 1981.

question becomes apparent when we look at the policy alternatives proposed by our three paradigms.

SYNOPSIS. The Conservative position holds that the free operation of supply and demand is the correct and most effective determinant of agricultural prices. Liberals most frequently argue that an agricultural market left to itself is subject to wild cyclical fluctuation; thus, a variety of government interventions are necessary to maintain reasonable order. Radicals, meanwhile, see the American farm problem as a case of government being manipulated by agribusiness with the result that government intervention has harmed both small farmers and ordinary consumers.

Anticipating the Arguments

● Why do Conservatives believe that most government efforts to help farmers by "artificially" raising crop prices actually hurt both farmers and consumers?

● What is the historical and economic foundation to the Liberal argument that farmers can't "depend" on unregulated farm markets?

● Why do Radicals believe that most farmers have been losers under both regulated and unregulated agricultural production in the United States?

The Conservative Argument

Discussions of the "American Farm Problem" almost always begin with a mistaken identification of what the problem really is. Most agricultural observers, and especially most economists writing on farm issues, suggest that there is something inherently unstable about American agriculture. Somehow, agriculture is presented as "proof" that the market economy simply does not work, that the free-market forces of supply and demand break down. Conservatives agree that there is indeed a farm problem; however, that problem begins and remains in Washington, D.C., not in the corn and wheat fields of the Midwest or the commodities markets in Chicago. In other words, the

American farm problem is not the result of some basic failure of the market. It is the failure of federal policy to allow the market forces to work.

POLICY FAILURE IN TIMES OF SURPLUS

Although many politicians and some economists may believe and act to the contrary, supply and demand remain the only effective determinants of prices and resource allocation. Of course, it is possible to contrive "desired" prices and output through a manipulated agricultural policy, but, regardless of short-run success, such policies must produce serious misallocations and costs in the long run.

For a considerable period of time, at least since World War I, most economists understood the American farm problem as a matter of rising productivity with comparatively stable or modestly increasing demand. The result in the marketplace was a general and persistent downward pressure on farm prices. The economic options under such conditions were either to let prices fall to whatever level they might reach or to maintain prices artificially. Due largely to political pressure from the farm lobby in the depressed 1930s the government devised a variety—really a potpourri—of farm programs to keep prices up and supposedly guarantee a living income to the American farmer. Tariffs were slapped on foreign farm products. Certain "basic" farm products were guaranteed a government-paid "parity" price well above the going market price. Bureaucrats worked out production controls and acreage allotments, with the curious economic aim of paying producers not to produce. Except for the interlude of World War II, when vast overseas demand for U.S. agricultural products briefly restored farm prosperity, farm prices have been held up only by government price manipulation.

As a result, Americans have paid much more for their food than was necessary, and they have paid more than they realized. Most Americans probably did not notice the higher prices. Due to the phenomenal productivity of American agriculture and the steadily rising standard of living in the United States, these artificially higher prices seemed quite tolerable. Food expenditures, as a share of total consumer purchases, actually declined in the postwar years.

However, few consumers realized that they were paying an additional price. Consumers are also taxpayers, and as such they had to bear the cost of expensive government subsidies paid to farmers and of maintaining the bureaucracy set up to administer various farm programs. By 1970 these expenses were directly costing $6.3 billion per year. Since the early 1930s they have cost over $100 billion. If the taxpayer cost of food is added to the consumer cost of food, we then get a clearer picture of our food bill. And, it is not as inexpensive as we might have imagined.

These artificial prices, moreover, interfered with the flow of human resources out of agriculture that otherwise might have been expected. The "gentle" Liberals were supposedly interested in cushioning the declining income of millions of American farmers. In fact, many of these farmers were functionally redundant. Many who might have moved off their relatively unproductive family farms were enticed to stay by the promise (but not reality) of higher farm incomes. These farmers, though unable to take advantage of increasingly expensive farm technology, stayed on their farms when, for their own benefit, they should have moved to other jobs.

Meanwhile, higher American farm prices closed off American food products from world markets. Due to climate, soil, technology, and agricultural science, American agriculture had an enormous advantage over the rest of the world in food production. This advantage and the export income it would have created was frittered away by programs aimed at keeping domestic prices relatively high. Precisely at a time when the United States faced a worsening balance of international payments (after World War II), the government pursued an agricultural program that denied the nation earnings it could have been making by exporting food.

ATTEMPTS AT A NEW POLICY DIRECTION

The chronic problem of agricultural overproduction began to dissipate in the early 1970s—no thanks to federal farm policy. In the early seventies the world faced a serious and growing food shortage. Population growth, increased spendable income around the world, and a number of calamitous droughts and crop failures created greater demand for American wheat, corn, soybeans, beef, and pork. The storage bins began to empty and farm prices rose, increasing by over 90 percent between 1967 and 1974.

The most important and also the most controversial development of this period was the massive sale of 19 million metric tons of grain to the Russians in 1972. For a number of years Soviet leadership had been yielding to consumer pressure to produce more meat protein. Of necessity, this meant providing greater amounts of grain for beef in feeding lots. When the 1971 and 1972 crops failed to reach expectations, the Soviet leaders decided not to slaughter their beef herds or tell their people to eat potatoes and beets. They chose instead to buy U.S. grain and to allow their "protein program" to continue.

The Russian purchase in 1972–1973 was not a one-shot affair. Some 8 million metric tons of grain were sold to the Soviet Union in 1974 and about 3 million tons the next year. The Russians experienced crop failures again in 1975 and negotiated another sale—this one for 13 million tons—for 1976. Although this sale was suspended temporarily when worldwide prospects of underproduction caused world and domestic grain prices to skyrocket, it was reinstituted when the bumper 1975 harvest came in. Meanwhile, the Soviet Union and the United States concluded long-term agreements for Russian purchase of 6 to 8 million tons of corn and wheat each year, with the American government reserving the right to curtail sales if reserves or domestic output fell too sharply.*

To growers and sellers, the "discovery" of the Russian market was a critical new direction for American agriculture, an end to the long era of chronic excess production, depressed prices, and dependence upon varieties of government subsidy programs. By selling the equivalent of one quarter of the 1972 crop, the Russian grain deal literally emptied American storage bins and grain elevators. This additional demand drove the prices of wheat from $1.70 per bushel in mid 1972 to $5.00 in 1973.

As farm "prosperity" returned, the first real change in government farm policy in over fifty years begain to take shape. Government finally got out of the business of buying and storing surplus production, and excessively high parity prices were replaced by more reasonable target prices. Although certainly not sweeping enough to satisfy most Conservatives, it seemed a first small step in the right direction, namely, getting government out of agriculture altogether.

Agriculture, however, has always been subject to changing short-term cycles. This year's high prices will cause next year's production to rise, shifting next year's supply upward faster than demand increases. The resulting lower prices lead to a gradual reduction of sup-

---

*During the "Afghan Crisis" in 1980, sales to the Russians were halted briefly.

ply over time until demand catches up—or at least it should work this way, if government does not interfere to hold prices up. This cyclical movement should not be seen as a "problem," for it is simply the way agricultural markets self-adjust. In fact, it is the way all markets work when they are free. Less than $600 million was doled out in price supports, just 10 percent the amount given away two years before.

By 1976 agricultural producers had increased greatly their supply and, as the law of supply and demand would have it, food prices began to level off and even come down a bit. While small variations in price will be common as supply and demand falter and rise from time to time, the variations will be a small price to pay for restoring market-directed order to agriculture. Yet practically any price downturn will produce cries of anguish from farmers long accustomed to Washington coming to their aid.

The political effort to withstand farm-interest-group pressures when periodic excess production or slack demand forces prices down demands great courage. Regrettably, the Carter administration did not show such strength in the passage of a new agricultural act in 1977. Instead of standing fast against the temporarily depressed agricultural prices, this legislation reinstituted target prices (the price government will guarantee farmers through subsidies regardless of the going market price they sell at). The supports for wheat, for instance, were set at between $.50 and $.75 above the market price prevailing then. With support prices about 25 percent above the market price for wheat—and similar increases in other supports—the 1978 pricetag to government (the taxpayers) was about $6 billion. And, naturally enough, the artificially high prices stimulated additional surplus production in 1978 and 1979. By 1982, outlays for price supports and farm subsidies had reached $12 billion.

A RAY OF HOPE

Despite our falling back from the early 1970s' promise of a gradual return to free agricultural markets, Conservatives have come to hope that reason will prevail eventually. The evidence clearly supports the view that less intervention produces greater benefits. *First,* farm income has increased significantly in the recent period of moderately relaxed government intervention (although it has been eroded a bit by high interest rates and recession in the past couple of years). Farm lobby arguments about "the poor, underpaid farmer" are much less convincing today when farm income is about 90 percent of non-farm income than they were in the early 1930s when it was less than one-third (see Table 1.1). The protesting farmers who drove around the streets of Washington, D.C. in the spring of 1979, tearing up asphalt with their $75,000 tractors, gained little popular or political support. The call by farm movement leaders to return to the New Deal program of paying 90 percent of "parity" prices fell on the deaf ears of a public that was beginning to recognize that "aid to the farmer" meant "distress to the consumer and taxpayer."

Second, farm productivity has continued to grow. Between 1970 and 1980, the farm population decreased by about 20 percent from 9.7 million to 7.8 million. Over the same period output rose by more than 25 percent; thus eliminating many of the old government interventions in agriculture has forced redundant resources out of agriculture and encouraged efficient farmers to increase their output.

Third, the continued growth of worldwide demand for food should mean moderately rising prices in the future. Such a long-term trend should reduce the periodic pressure to apply "quick-fix" band-aids when short-run periods of distress appear.

Fourth, a healthy and self-reliant agricultural sector—not one dependent upon government handouts—is becoming increasingly important to the overall economic strength of the American economy. As Figure 1.2 shows, the value of farm exports has simply exploded over the past decade. Agricultural products are the nation's largest

Table 1.1   Farm Income as a Percent of Nonfarm Income in the United States, 1934–1980

1934	32%
1937	44%
1940	36%
1944	55%
1948	68%
1952	59%
1956	47%
1960	54%
1965	68%
1970	74%
1975	88%
1980	91%

Source: Calculated from U.S. Department of Agriculture, *Farm Income Statistics*, 1981.

FIGURE 1.2   U.S. AGRICULTURE EXPORTS, 1962–1980

Year

Source: U.S. Department of Agriculture, 1981.

single export item. Whether Americans realize it or not, a revitalized agricultural sector is our best, and perhaps our only, hedge against Arab oil "stickups" and the dwindling efficiency of our nonagricultural production. Looked at this way, the importance of ending agricultural reliance upon government and ending inefficiency and resource dislocation in agriculture is all the more important.

The Liberal Argument

Conservatives are quite right in pointing out that the American farm problem has been largely one of gains in production consistently outstripping increases in demand. Throughout most of this century, food demand was essentially a function of domestic population increase. Until recently the United States has exported large quantities of food abroad only in time of war. Meanwhile, steady advances in agricultural technology and science have produced greater output, reducing human employment. Table 1.2 puts these gains in perspective.

Table 1.2   U.S. Agricultural Productivity, 1800–1950

Crop	1800	1880	1920	1950
Wheat				
yield/acre (bu)	15	13	14	17
labor hours/100 bu	373	152	87	28
Corn				
yield/acre (bu)	25	26	28	39
labor hours/100 bu	344	180	113	39
Cotton				
yield/acre (bu)	147	179	160	283
labor hours/bale	601	318	269	126

Source: U.S. Bureau of the Census, *Historical Statistics of the United States*, Series K 83–97 (Washington, D.C., 1960).

RISING PRODUCTION AND GROWING CRISIS

Each unit of land has been producing greater yields as a result of new fertilizers and hybrid strains. At the same time, the application of greater capital has reduced substantially the number of manhours needed in production. By the 1930s American farmers were the most productive in the world—and also going broke the fastest. It is easy enough for the Conservative devotee of the laws of supply and demand to say, "Leave things alone and let the devil take the hindmost." The fact is, excess agricultural production and falling prices affected people—a great number of people.

In 1930 about 44 percent of the American population was still classified as rural. About 57 million people still lived on farms or in small towns dependent on agriculture. At least 31 million were full-time farmers. To have adopted the Conservative proposal of letting these human resources "drop out" of farming if it didn't pay and find alternative employment would have been inhumane and stupid. In the Great Depression decade, there was no alternative employment. The exodus from farming (which did reduce the farm population to less than 10 million by 1972) would have been faster and would have created even greater employment problems for the general economy.

With this in mind, the New Deal policies of reducing farm migration through price supports, direct payments, and other subsidies (easy credit, electrification, and so on) were created. To be sure, these programs *did* artificially hold up farm prices and, in terms of subsidy costs, *did* pass the cost of the farm program on to taxpayers at large.

But they also brought a degree of order to the agricultural sector and improved the income distribution inequities between farmers and nonfarmers. For example, in 1934 farm income was only about one-third that of nonfarm income ($163 per year per person compared to $469 per year per person). By 1964, after nearly thirty years of New Deal-type "tinkering," annual farm income per person stood at $1,405 and nonfarm income at $2,318. Moreover, the supposed costs of federal farm subsidy programs have been vastly overstated. The $6.3 billion paid in 1970 was less than one-tenth of all federally paid subsidies to the private sector; of this total about $4 billion was paid out for just three agricultural products—feed grains, wheat, and cotton.

Before concluding this topic, it must be conceded that past American agricultural policy has had its failures. For instance, the improved income situation of the farm sector, a noteworthy achievement, masks some other problems. The farm programs of the 1930s, 1940s, and 1950s could not halt the eventual decline of the family farm or the regional small farm in the Northeast. With greater application of technology and changes in farm production, farm employment (mostly family workers) fell from 7 million in 1960 to 4.5 million in 1977. Although average farm income did improve relative to nonfarm income during the 1960s and 1970s, maldistribution of earnings within the farm sector increased.

As Figure 1.3 shows, the large farms ($100,000 or more per year of gross income) grew from a 17.3 percent share of farm earnings in 1960 to a 58.2 percent share in 1980. These figures are even more impressive when we look at the number of farms in each income category. As the data show, these large enterprises amount to only 7.5 percent of all farms. Over 75 percent of American farms are comparatively small (gross earnings of less than $40,000).

We easily can conclude then that the few big farms have been getting bigger but that most remaining farmers still earn very modest incomes. In such a situation, it is quite likely that past farm subsidy programs and payments for nonproduction have provided the greatest gains for the large farm producer. However, even with such shortcomings, the earlier farm policies are defensible. They did raise and maintain average farm earnings above what a purely laissez-faire solution would have produced, thus strengthening agriculture in general. They mitigated the impact of the Depression on many farmers, and when farm out-migration did occur after World War II, it was more easily

FIGURE 1.3   THE RISE OF LARGE FARMS, 1960–1980

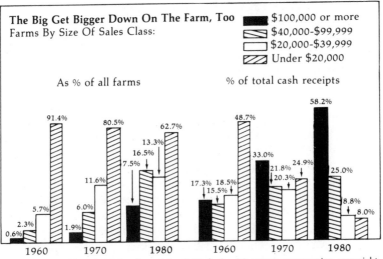

Source: Reprinted by permission from *Sales & Marketing Management* magazine, copyright 1977. U.S. Department of Agriculture, *Farm Income Statistics,* 1981.

absorbed into a growing economy. The Conservatives' laissez-faire policy would have emptied rural America sooner, encouraged the growth of only the largest farms, and led to unacceptable human costs.

While past Liberal farm policies are historically defensible, it is apparent that America has moved into a new agricultural era demanding policy changes. The capital-intensive nature of agriculture is everywhere apparent, and the day of the small family farm has passed. At the same time, the long-run future growth in world food demand is undeniable. These trends, however, are misunderstood by the free-market advocates.

DEVELOPING A NEW FARM PROGRAM

Between 1972 and 1975, agricultural prices generally rose. As long as that was the case, price supports and any effort to restrict output were unnecessary and ill-advised. However, as the Agriculture and Consumer Protection Act of 1973 anticipated, high prices paid to farmers would not hold permanently. The 1973 act, renewed and expanded in 1977 and again in 1981, introduced the concept of target pricing. Under this arrangement, government announces a target price on a specified list of commodities. If the market price is below the target price, the government pays the farmer the difference between what they would receive for selling their goods in the market and the targeted figure. According to such a plan, consumers would still enjoy the benefits of the lower market price, but farms would be guaranteed a reasonable return on their crops. To prevent the very large producers from tapping the public treasury for outrageous subsidy payments, the 1973 law specified that no farmer should receive more than $20,000 in payment for any crop.

The Liberals' expectation that pure supply and demand solutions to the agricultural problem would fail were proven by 1977, as farm prices fell precipitously. The agricultural act of that year updated the target prices to adjust for inflation and again provided a floor to farm income. Many farmers argued that the floor was too low. Farmers demonstrated in Washington, and held mildly effective strikes; but the farm sector was protected from the far greater agonies that a Conservative free-market program would have created. This, however, is not the last word on the farm problem. In addition to these recent policy changes, others might be considered. For instance, a crop reserve should be established. This would provide a market for certain storable crops in good years as a hedge against drastic price increases in bad times. Finally, farmers might need some help as prices for machinery, fertilizer, and the like continue to rise. This could mean direct government action against monopolistically maintained supplier prices or provision for low-cost loans to help farmers pay for these items.

The Conservative focus on the long-run trends in agricultural markets is misleading and their argument for "free" agricultural markets is simpleminded. A long-run trend is nothing more than the average of a cycle of short-run highs and lows. If the short-run fluctuations are extreme, especially the lows, the agricultural sector will be torn apart. Resources forced out of agriculture in bad periods will not return quickly when prices later rise. A farm is not an enterprise that can be worked for a few years and then briefly retired until the boom "naturally" reappears. The land "blows away" if it isn't cultivated and the equipment rusts and becomes obsolete. Neither the farmer nor the consumer, who would face violently fluctuating prices, should be subjected to the severity of short-run market readjustments. The laws of supply and demand, in fact, can be regulated to improve market outcomes.

The Radical Argument

When conventional economics textbooks reach for an example in discussions of "how supply and demand sets prices" or "how competition works," agricultural markets usually are cited. In the idealized models, at least, there are many small producers and consumers of homogeneous products, haggling and bargaining until a fair and equitable price is established. For anyone faintly familiar with the real-world conditions of American agriculture, the irony is heavy; nothing could be further from the truth. Perhaps because we start with such subtle deceptions when we talk about agricultural markets, we continue to deceive ourselves when we look for solutions to real farm problems. At any rate, American agricultural affairs are dominated by a comparatively small number of giant producers, not by many small equal-sized farms; and prices are more the result of market power or government intervention than of the free market at work. Agriculture, as much as any sector of the economy, reveals the conflict between the professed ideals of a modified, production-for-profit system and the reality that a few benefit at the losses of many. The losers, of course, are small farmers and consumers in general.

THE OLD POLICY: HELP THE BIG GUYS

While most farm programs between 1920 and 1973 were supposedly aimed at protecting the family farm and supporting the agricultural sector in general, they utterly failed to halt the concentration of agriculture into fewer and fewer hands. Programs of price supports and payments for nonproduction stimulated this concentration, since small farmers could not possibly reap many gains from them. Between 1930 and 1980, land under cultivation actually increased, but the number of farms declined from 6.5 to 2.4 million. While Liberals reluctantly note this tendency, they do not understand that it has meant higher prices to consumers with few, if any, benefits to most individually owned farms.

The market power of farmers, never very strong anyway, was eroded further during the 1950s and 1960s as marketing procedures were affected increasingly by the entrance of large business corporations into agriculture—*agribusiness*. Food chains bought orchards and feedlots and integrated their operations all the way from the planting and slaughtering to the store checkout counter. Cereal producers, dairy product firms, baking companies, and other farm purchasers became more concentrated. At the same time suppliers of farm machinery became increasingly integrated. As a result, farmers paid high, monopoly-established prices for equipment and had to sell their produce to a comparatively few buyers. These buyers rarely had to pay more than the support price or "take-it-or-leave-it" prices for nonsupported commodities. Contract production with big companies replaced the old market relationships. For instance, half of all fresh vegetables are grown under contract.

By the early 1970s, agriculture had been "discovered" by the large industrial conglomerates. Agribusiness grew and matured as ITT absorbed Wonder Bread and Smithfield Hams, Ling-Temco-Vought took control of Wilson Meats, Greyhound joined with Armour Packing, and other similar mergers took place. Basically, this phenomenon extended and accentuated the "price taker" situation of American farmers, even large farmers. Whether selling to the government, A&P, or General Foods, farmers had long been accustomed to dealing with buyers who set their own prices. The real power of this new and rejuvenated agribusiness, however, would be felt by the consumer as well. The new conglomerate middlemen in food production and distribution had the potential capacity to extract enormous profits. By 1972 the structure for increasing food prices and middlemen's profits had been laid down. The only restraint was that posed by general overproduction in American agriculture. The Russian grain deal soon changed this situation. By eliminating both the fact and the psychology of overproduction and comparatively low prices in agricultural goods, the deal paved the way for agribusiness to assert its power over table food prices.

In 1972 the United States and the Soviet Union secretly negotiated the sale of 19 million metric tons of American grain. Ironically, this sale was completed precisely as the United States was mining Haiphong Harbor in North Vietnam and bombing rail lines north of Hanoi in an effort to stop the flow of Russian goods into the war zone.

Although critics were to attack the sale as the "Great Grain Robbery," Secretary of Agriculture Earl Butz defended it as a boon to the American farmer. When accused of being willing to trade with the devil if it meant a profit, Butz replied, "If he has dollars."

THE NEW POLICY: KEEP PRICES UP

The Russian grain deal actually reflected a highly calculated effort at creating superprofits out of the anguish of farmers and the general public. Since the government itself lacked the legal authority to export goods, the grain sales had to be consummated by some half-dozen leading American grain-trading firms. The steps in the selling process were something like this: First, the harvest came in and could not be altered by farmer action. Second, the Department of Agriculture's Commodity Credit Corporation (CCC) granted the Russians exceptionally low credit arrangements. Third, the companies purchased the wheat owned and stored by the government in CCC bins and sold it to the Russians at a price significantly below the prevailing domestic price. Fourth, the companies, over and above their sales fees, received millions in subsidies from the government (the difference between the domestic price and the sale price).

The effects of the sales were injurious to practically all Americans except the grain companies and a few insiders who were able to make extraordinary profits by speculating on grain futures. Farmers were unable to take advantage of the resulting rise in wheat prices, since most had sold their grain to the government at the going market price. The American grain reserve was eliminated. Wheat prices and prices of substitute products went up, and so did the prices of beef and bread, both dependent upon grain prices. Restive consumers were told it was just the law of supply and demand.

The Conservative prediction that growing world agricultural sales would eventually bring prosperity back to farming, although creating some hope in 1973–1974, had turned to ashes by 1978. Four years after Secretary Butz promised a new era for farming by opening American agriculture to the world, farmers had become dependent on world demand to get rid of two-thirds of their wheat, one quarter of their corn, and half their soybeans. While American overseas grain sales remained fairly high, world grain prices (indeed, most world agricultural prices) tumbled.

Did lower farm prices translate into significantly lower food prices? Hardly. With large food corporations and agribusiness controlling the final goods prices for most U.S. food consumption, lowered per-unit farm prices meant higher profits, not lower prices at the grocery store. Food processors and distributors (who received on the average 65¢ of every food dollar) saw their revenues and profits soar, as farmers groaned and consumers cursed. Consumers blamed farmers. Farmers blamed unions for rising equipment costs, and Arabs for higher energy and fertilizer bills. Almost no one has placed the responsibility where it really belongs—with the grain trading companies and their agents at the Department of Agriculture and with agribusiness monopolies, which are well represented in Washington.

Those who argue that world population pressures and scarcity are the cause of higher food prices are simply not telling the truth. During the past decade the United States has reduced the amount of food it makes available annually for the Food for Peace program (directed at the starving nations). It sells less to the poor nations, precisely as it sells more to fatten Russian beef. High food prices do not reflect absolute or relative scarcity of food, but superprofits by agribusiness. Any program attempting to unravel the food-price problem must begin by directing its attention at the real culprits—American business, or at least the part of it that dominates food production and pricing. The high cost of eating is not explained by the Conservatives' "magical" supply-and-demand curves.

WHAT STRATEGY TO DEAL WITH THE PROBLEM?

From the Radical perspective, the Farm Problem has a number of different and troublesome dimensions. First of all, the chronic tendency toward overproduction and falling prices followed by underproduction and rising prices simply reflects the instability and irrationality of "free" markets. The vicious cycle that sometimes brings prosperity and sometimes crisis can be mitigated only by an effort to plan output and control prices. The trouble is that past control efforts have been biased toward helping the large farmer and agribusiness at the expense of the small farmer. As Table 1.3 indicates, the share of government support payments going to giant enterprises has been growing. Farms with sales over $40,000 per year received 34 percent

Table 1.3   The Big Farmers Get More and More

Size and Distribution	1970	1979
$100,000 and over sales		
% of farms	1.9	7.0
% of government support payments	14.2	21.5
$40,000 to 100,000 sales		
% of farms	6.1	14.6
% of government support payments	19.4	36.0
$20,000 to 40,000 sales		
% of farms	11.1	12.9
% of government support payments	22.7	21.5
Less than $20,000 sales		
% of farms	76.1	66.3
% of government support payments	43.7	21.0

Source: U.S. Department of Agriculture, *Farm Income Statistics*, July 1979.

of all government payments in 1970. By 1979, they received 57 percent.

Such a payment schedule tends to encourage overproduction among the large farms while at the same time pushing the small producer to the wall. By 1983, one-third of all farms, mostly small ones, were delinquent on their debts. Reversing the direction of payments would equalize income but encourage inefficient farm producers to continue operations. The Gordian Knot can be untied only if we develop an output and pricing program that humanely moves inefficient agricultural producers out of production while at the same time curbing the ability of the giant farm enterprises to set output and prices for their own—but not the consumer's—advantage.

Also, the other half of giant farming's ability to "double dip" must cease. Presently, agribusiness gets *both* higher prices *and* transfers. The ordinary citizen pays twice. Often the taxpayers pay a producer not to produce. Those who would argue that pricing and output controls proposed by Radicals create inefficiency should explain how payment for nonproduction is efficient.

Meanwhile, policy regulating agribusiness and middleman processing profits is also essential. The tendency for food prices to remain high while farm prices fall can be explained only in terms of maintaining unjustified profits at the processing, transporting, or retail levels. Thus far, all farm policies—both Conservative market solutions or

Liberal transfer payment systems—have avoided confronting a fact that every homemaker knows: There is precious little correlation between falling agricultural prices and the price of a market basket of food.

Such short-term strategies as boycotts of grocery chains have not been effective. Choosing not to eat simply doesn't work against food prices in the long run. As a tactic for mass political organization, it may be a useful educational experience, a lesson that can be applied later in more effective ways; however, the long-run solution requires a system of allocating and pricing that is totally inconsistent with our historical approach to agriculture and food production. The "unthinkable"—social control of production and prices—must be thought about. As we shall see, it is an approach that should not be limited simply to the farm problem.

ISSUE 2

Consumer Protection
The Matter of Automobile Safety

Consumption is the sole end and the purpose of all production;
and the interest of the producer ought to be attended to, only in
so far as it may be necessary for promoting that of the consumer.

Adam Smith, 1776

The upshot of consumer protection, when it succeeds, is simply
to hold industry to higher standards of excellence, and I can't see
why they should object to that kind of incentive

Ralph Nader, 1967

Let me emphasize: competition does not protect the consumer
because businessmen are more softhearted than bureaucrats or
because they are more altruistic or because they are more gener-
ous, but only because it is in the self-interest of the entrepreneur
to protect the consumer.

Milton Friedman, 1978

Originally, the idea of consuming more and better things was
meant to give man a happier, more satisfied life. Consumption
was a means to an end, that of happiness. It now has become an
aim in itself.

Erich Fromm, 1955

THE PROBLEM

According to the time-honored doctrine of consumer sovereignty, the final authority in determining production and prices is the consumer. In this view, consumers vote with their dollars in the marketplace. Their decisions, presumably intelligently formed, are expressed by their final selection and willingness to pay for goods. Since the mid 1960s, however, the theory of consumer sovereignty has been challenged by *consumerism*—the consumer protection movement.

To consumer protectionists, consumer sovereignty is really *caveat emptor*, let the buyer beware. Their argument, in simple terms, holds that consumers cannot possibly know the quality or possible detrimental effects of the goods they purchase. Consumer demand is manipulated by television, advertising, and an uncritical desire to "keep up with the Joneses" by copying other people's consumption habits. Accordingly, consumers have become increasingly exploited by sellers of shoddy and dangerous commodities.

The consumerist movement was launched in 1965 with the publication of Ralph Nader's *Unsafe at any Speed*, an effective muckraking attack on a popular General Motors car, the Corvair. Nader argued persuasively that the sporty rear-engined auto had a number of defects, among them a dangerous habit of flipping over when cornering, even at low speeds. He also claimed that General Motors engineers and managers knew about the car's engineering deficiencies but had kept quiet about them. Corvair sales dropped after Nader's attack, although General Motors disputed his influence. The company made its last Corvair in 1969.

Spurred by Nader and his activists and by the sobering fact that auto fatalities had grown by about 1 percent a year since 1960, Congress enacted the National Traffic and Auto Safety Act in 1966. This legislation required that the auto industry begin to install certain specific safety features in all new cars. The first requirements (which went into effect in 1968) specified seatbelts for all occupants, energy-absorbing steering columns, increased windshield resistance, dual braking systems, and padded instrument panels. Over the years, additional safety requirements have been mandated by the National Highway Safety and Traffic Safety Administration (also established in 1966) and many others are "on the drawing board."

Meanwhile, Nader's consumer advocate activities soon spread to other areas, and his popularity and political effectiveness grew. Within a few years, state and federal laws were introduced to give consumers greatly expanded power in product-liability and class-action suits. By 1975 over a million such suits were being initiated each year. More important, perhaps, has been the creation of new consumer protection agencies. The Federal Trade Commission now includes a Bureau of Consumer Protection and a Bureau of Deceptive Practices. The executive branch boasts a special Assistant for Consumer Affairs and a Consumer Advisory Council. By 1976 over 400 separate units in forty different government agencies were operating to advance consumer interests or protect consumer rights.

Although opinion surveys of American consumers report broad popular support for most consumer protection activities, the movement has run into trouble recently. Consumer protection, of course, costs money—in the form of higher costs for safer products and in the form of expanded government payrolls for consumer protectionists. After the Conservative Reagan victory in 1980, both those cost elements came under increasing attack. Having pledged itself to roll back government regulation in all areas of economic life, the administration returned to the scene of the original "consumer protection crime"—automobiles. For the American automobile industry, hard hit by a deep recession in 1981–1982 and by a flood of cheaper foreign imports, the Reagan administration provided a virtual freeze on pending speedometer, passive-restraint, bumper, windshield, and 35-MPH crash-rating requirements. GM pointed out that the resulting savings, along with the relaxed automobile emission standards, would give the company an extra half-million to a million dollars a day to regroup and to face hard times and the Japanese. Consumer advocates cried "foul." Clearly, after more than a decade and a half of victories, the consumer movement was on the defense.

SYNOPSIS. Conservatives argue that consumers are best able to determine for themselves what they should buy and that efforts to "improve" upon consumer rationality diminishes satisfaction, raises prices, and lowers economic efficiency. Liberals maintain that consumers do not have enough strength to protect themselves from the manipulative power of giant enterprises. Radicals go beyond mere "consumer protection," raising questions about the commitment of the society to consume uncritically as an end in itself.

Anticipating the Arguments

- How do the Conservative, Liberal, and Radical views differ regarding the consumer's rationality and ability to choose freely and intelligently?

- In what ways do the Liberal and Conservative views of calculating the "cost" of goods differ?

- Why are Radicals suspicious of all efforts to "protect" consumers in a production-for-profit economic system?

The Conservative Argument

How safe should an automobile be? How safe can it be? Should all cars be built like M-16 tanks? Should speed limits be reduced to a much safer twenty miles per hour? Indeed, wouldn't the safest car be no car at all? We have started from a fairly intelligent question and proceeded to absurdity. And that is precisely the direction of the recent consumerist thrust into auto safety.

The past decade's agitation by a few consumer groups and rulings by growing layers of federal and state bureaucracies have forced auto makers to undertake serious engineering changes in car production. From seat belts to bumpers to impact-resistant frames, automobile manufacturers have had to meet a series of deadlines in installing safety devices. If we were in a joking mood, we might wonder how a satirist like Bob Newhart would have handled a crowd of consumer safety advocates a hundred years ago if they had turned their attention to the horse. The trouble is that the auto safety freaks—and practically all consumer advocates—are not funny. In point of fact, they are an economic and social expense. They interfere with the free functioning of supply and demand and infringe on social and individual freedoms.

THE ECONOMIC EFFECT

The required installation of automobile safety equipment adds to the cost of cars. Only believers in the tooth fairy would argue otherwise. GM, for instance, estimates that the required safety devices account for 10 percent of the production costs of an average automobile. These rising costs have had two important undesirable effects, one affecting consumers and one affecting the automobile industry.

Since most studies have shown that automobile demand is moderately elastic, the rising price of cars must reduce total sales. Many consumers will hold on to their present cars longer, own fewer family cars, or shift to alternative means of transportation that may be less desirable but cheaper. Moreover, rising automobile pricetags mean that consumers must rearrange their preferences so that, to get a needed car, they will forgo some other commodity. Higher priced cars actually may be traded off against clothes or even food. As a result, consumer well-being is actually lowered.

Meanwhile, auto safety requirements (and environmental controls) have nearly strangled the American auto industry. With sales down 40 percent or more from their mid-1970 highs, all American automakers have consistently reported losses during the early 1980s. Even giant GM has been staggering; but the losses at Chrysler, Ford, and AMC eventually may be fatal. Thus, auto safety not only raises prices, lowers demand, and reduces overall corporate profitability, but also may have the wholly undesired effect of increasing industrial concentration in the automaking business. As we shall argue later, such undesired monopoly effects are almost always the result of interference with the market mechanism rather than of a latent tendency within business.

In addition to adding direct costs to consumers and producers, consumer protection increases taxes. Federal and state protection agencies spend about $4 billion each year to administer their programs. These, of course, are also direct costs, but they often are overlooked when we total up the consumer protection bill.

THE SOCIAL EFFECT

The decision to enforce most automobile safety standards denies consumers the right to own unsafe autos if they want to. Safety standards to protect third parties—pedestrians and other drivers—are probably justifiable on the grounds of community protection. But the thrust of practically all safety efforts have been aimed at car owners and occupants (who are there, after all, as a matter of choice). The owner who wants safety should be able to buy it—collapsible steering wheels, padded dashboards, air bags, and the whole works. However, the consumer who values personal safety less than some other purchase should be free to make the choice. How far is enforced self-protection to go? Will each home have a food inspector peering into the kitchen pots and checking the cholesterol and fat intake? Beyond the obvious economic effect of making consumers pay more and thus compelling them to rearrange their budget choices, rigid automobile safety standards subtract from personal freedom.

The dismal record of consumers' voluntary interest in automobile safety is fairly well documented. When the Ford Motor Company voluntarily added certain safety options to its cars in the 1950s, it met with public apathy. There was no rush to buy cars with seat belts and padded dashes. Ford quickly abandoned its experiment. Meanwhile, National Safety Council surveys of automobile seat-belt usage indicate that less than half of all drivers and occupants use them regularly. Although speed limits have been lowered and are observed by many drivers (because of fuel costs, not safety), speeding remains such a serious problem that New York State recently organized a $6-million state police task force to enforce speed laws. Quite simply, broad social concern for automobile safety is nonexistent.

A DIGRESSION ON COST-BENEFIT

A frequently cited proof of the efficacy of automobile safety rules is that the fatality and injury rates have fallen since the passage of the Vehicle Safety Act of 1966. While Conservatives will accept the fact of lowered fatalities, they believe that it deserves careful study before concluding a causal connection with enforced safety standards. Indeed, a recent American Enterprise Institute study has pointed out that factors other than safety devices may explain this trend.

For instance, the age profile of the population might be considered. The birth rate peaked around 1950, and this led to a slower growth of under-twenty-five-year-old drivers, the most accident-prone age group. Also, we might look at income and cost trends. Since the late 1960s, real income growth has slowed and the cost of repairs and medical bills has risen greatly. Would not these tendencies act as a deterrent to risk taking while driving? We might also ask: Have driving patterns changed so as to reduce travel and risk, especially with the rising price of gasoline? A whole range of additional factors similar to these might be considered. What have been the effects of smaller cars, radial tires, new highways, driver education, and so on?

The point of this digression should be obvious. The well-known Liberal argument that social benefits of reduced injury and death outweigh the dollar cost of safety equipment simply cannot be proved so long as there is no way to be certain that the safety equipment has had any significant effect on the reduction of injuries and death. The true value of safety equipment cannot be ascertained.

Ironically, from a social point of view, the automobile safety movement may produce the opposite of its desired results: Automobile safety in fact may decline. Indeed, it could be argued (but not proved) that safety equipment actually could increase accidents since drivers with supposedly safer cars would be willing to take increased chances while driving.

Meanwhile, as the price of automobiles increases and consumers (at least the majority, with an elastic demand for cars) determine to forgo new-car purchases, older and less-safe machines will make up a larger share of the nation's private vehicles. The repair expense to keep an old car on the road is now less than the expense of buying a new car. Regardless of federal indifference to supply and demand in its automobile safety programs, federal authority cannot repeal all the laws of market behavior. To be sure, the government could enact more stringent inspection requirements for old vehicles, but human ingenuity and a few dollars to friendly gas station inspectors would likely blunt tighter inspection efforts. Meanwhile, whether successful or not, the inspection effort would represent one more layer of bureaucratic control.

We can see, therefore, that consumerist programs do not improve on the market's own defense of "consumer sovereignty." The Conservative position is to halt government interference. The best program is no consumer program. Happily, the consumer movement trend seems to have peaked. The costs, both economic and personal, are being recognized. In the growing mood of deregulation of the economy, it is reasonable to hope that we shall turn back from the false assumption that government can and will protect us better than we can protect ourselves.

The Liberal Argument

The classical economic assumption—that buyers and sellers bargain equally in the marketplace and that buyers, acting with restraint and wisdom, are sovereign—falls into the same intellectual category as belief that the world is flat. As in the case of the "flat worlders," a great many compelling reasons can be mustered to "prove" the argument, but they fly in the face of virtually all available evidence.

From the Liberal point of view, interference in the private production of goods is justifiable and necessary for several reasons. First of all, average consumers have had great difficulty in obtaining accurate information about the goods they buy. Almost daily, the Food and Drug Administration and other research-oriented government and private agencies reveal a new atrocity: Thalidomide, Red Dye No. 2, Tris, and so on. These goods have been sold or used without the consumer's knowledge of their effects.

Second is the matter of *external costs*—costs paid by the society that may not be accounted for in the selling price of a good. Conservatives consider only the private cost of an automobile: how much an individual must pay in the marketplace for a minimally equipped transportation vehicle. Additional costs for safety features again are seen as purely private purchasing decisions: buy safety if *you* want it. This misses an important point in understanding real costs. Automobiles have a cost that goes beyond merely the production, assembly, and sales expenditures and the expected profits of the automaker. The private decision to drive an unsafe but cheaper car means that society pays an additional bill for the costs inflicted on others by automobile accidents. Auto accidents, however, affect more people than those who are injured. They lead to higher insurance rates; greater court costs; and heavier expenditures on roads, accident prevention, and enforcement. Nor are injuries or deaths simply "personal" matters. These human losses mean the dollar loss of present wage earnings and the loss of productive workers (now and in the future), and thus a greatly expanded social cost to the whole society.

Thus, the Conservatives' argument against automobile safety standards on the ground that they unfairly raise consumer costs misses the whole point. Higher-priced autos are necessary to cover all the costs involved in auto driving. As we shall see, it is still a good bargain.

SPEED VERSUS SAFETY

The extraordinary growth of giant enterprises over the past century, along with the development of huge advertising budgets and sophisticated selling techniques, has created immense power on the sellers' side of the market. Economic concentration has given producers great freedom in establishing and maintaining their own price and quality standards. Massive advertising, meanwhile, has moved well beyond an informational function to one of actually creating and manipulating consumer wants. In such a situation, it is essential that government intervene on behalf of consumers to protect them from false advertising and poorly made or dangerous merchandise.

The past decade's efforts in the areas of automobile safety are an example of how govermentally supported consumer protection actions can improve the quality of an important consumer good. Outside of a house, a car is usually the largest single outlay made by a consumer. Americans own about 120 million cars. Once considered a rich man's luxury (and, after the Model T, the poor man's luxury), today the auto has become everyone's necessity. The vast majority of citizens are dependent on the auto to get to work, school, stores, and many recreational activities.

However, just as consumers began to buy more and more cars after World War II, the automakers began to shift consumer attention from a car's serviceability and economy to its size, horsepower, and styling. (This trend actually had begun with General Motors in the early 1930s, but depression, war, and generally poor highways did not allow it to blossom until the late 1940s and 1950s.) The "ideal" car became one with speed, internal comfort, and annual style changes that could quickly distinguish it from last year's model or from other manufacturer's offerings. While social critics sneered at Americans' fancies and fantasies in automobiles, very few paid much attention to safety hazards. Autos had probably never been very safe, but by 1965, 55,000 Americans were dying each year on the roads. New highways, along with greater horsepower and more weight, had made automobiles lethal weapons. The auto industry, which had shrunk from ten producers to just four, paid no attention to safety standards. Their advertising and their research emphasized speed and comfort, and the buying public had accepted these values. Until Ralph Nader and a few others focused attention on safety inadequacies, rarely did car dealers have to respond to queries about how safe their products were.

In the past decade, all this has changed. Government, working through Congress and administrative rulings by new protection agencies (such as the National Highway Safety Administration), created minimum safety requirements for all cars: safety belts, bumper improvements, window defrosters, stronger glass, and the like. Careful monitoring of autos has led to massive recalls to remedy specific safety deficiencies. Speed, the great killer in most cases, has been deemphasized in product advertising. The latter development has of course been aided by the rising cost of gasoline, which has induced consumers to value performance over horsepower.

THE SAVINGS FROM SAFETY

Government safety requirements have no doubt added to the price of automobiles, although much less than the industry has argued. Safety belts, for instance, which (when used) have radically reduced serious injuries in collisions, add less than 1 percent to the price of a $9,000 automobile. The problem, of course, is to measure the increases in costs to consumers against the savings to society from reduced auto hazards. It would be inaccurate to stress only increased auto prices in a survey of auto safety costs and benefits.

Using the crudest kind of calculation, the dollar costs per year of automobile safety could be estimated as high as $4.5 billion. This is based upon GM's own 1982 calculation that the various safety mandates (not to be confused with environmental requirements) added $500 to each car's production cost and further assumes average sales to be 9 million cars. The benefits are more difficult to calculate. We do know, though, that each life unnecessarily lost is also a loss to society in earned wages for the period of the victim's work life. We also know from available auto safety statistics that auto-related deaths have declined by about 10,000 per year since the first significant safety features were added to the 1969-model cars. Using a recent U.S. Department of Transportation "interrupted earning stream" estimate of

$500,000 value per victim's life and calculating that at least three-quarters of the 10,000 reductions in fatalities is the direct or indirect result of improved safety standards, we can demonstrate at least $3.7 billion in social savings from reduced fatalities alone. Additional savings from reduced or less serious injuries and the psychological gratification of feeling safer in one's auto would more than cover the liberally estimated dollar cost of the safety equipment. In a more complicated and extensive benefits model, the U.S. Department of Transportation has estimated that presently mandated auto requirements would reduce fatalities by 24,000 by 1990, producing social savings of $9.5 billion. Doubtless, other models could be constructed, but even the most conservative should prove easily that auto safety pays for itself. Consumer protection isn't free, but it is a bargain.

Meanwhile, manufacturers complain that enforced recalls of cars to remedy defects constitutes an assault on their profits, and there is probably some truth to this. The answer to the problem, however, is better workmanship and engineering on the industry's part, not relaxed consumer protection. The cost for shoddy construction must be borne by industry, not by society at large.

If there is any serious defect in the government's efforts to protect car buyers, it is that not enough has been done. The Highway Safety Bureau, for instance, operates on a yearly budget of about $100 million and employs a staff of about 1000. That is a very small bureaucracy indeed to watch over safety standards in the nation's largest consumer-oriented industry.

The recent trend toward deregulation will cost the nation dearly if it continues. Conservatives are right in saying that withdrawing safety and consumer protection standards (and environmental and job-safety standards as well) could lead to lower-priced goods or, more realistically, greater industry profits. Conceivably such deregulation could give a sluggish economy a quick fix for a time. But these are cruel and false gains obtained only through "creative accounting"—by shifting the social or external cost of goods onto certain groups in the society. Greater efforts in auto safety as well as protection in other areas of consumer interest are essential. Consumer protection will not be attained until *caveat emptor* is replaced by *caveat venditor* (let the seller beware) as the dominant motto of the marketplace.

The Radical Argument

The relevant issues in the controversy over improved automobile safety are rarely raised. Conservatives approach the question as a matter of maintaining free markets and free choice, and Liberals argue for the improvement of market conditions and the protection of buyers; but these are really evasions of what the auto safety question highlights. Why, in an advanced and supposedly civilized society such as ours, is automobile safety a problem at all? Is it that we lack the resources and the technology to build safe vehicles? On the contrary, we all know that technology has nothing to do with the problem. Unsafe autos, like unsafe food and dangerous drugs, are just "there." They are part of our economic and social system—to be tolerated or, when things get bad enough, to be reformed. Auto hazards and the like are the necessary but unwanted effects of an irrational social order.

WHY "CONSUMER SOVEREIGNTY" DOESN'T EXIST

Capitalist economic systems are organized to make profits, not to make people happy or to make life safer. For a capitalist enterprise to make large profits, it has to sell in quantity, and it must obtain as great a surplus over costs as possible. Obviously that simple calculation nowhere contains any estimate of social costs and benefits. Insofar as the production-for-profit system is concerned, satisfaction is maximized simply if we have *more*. Irrespective of the time-honored tradition of consumer sovereignty, it is not really the consumers' power to choose among goods that is important. What is important is that they consume, period. Citizens in a capitalist society are taught from birth to accept uncritically that the object of life is to obtain goods; the more goods, the better their lives.

Looked at this way, it is easy to see why modern capitalism periodically becomes absorbed in such developments as the auto-safety issue. The social costs of the mass consumption of dangerous automobiles and even private concern about the problem have finally developed to such a point where reformist action must be taken. The auto-safety movement is merely another step in the long progression of product reform movements. It differs very little from the public outcry against adulterated food which created the Food and Drug Administration in 1906. The FDA certainly has improved food cleanliness, and probably the current consumer movement will make cars safer to drive (or at least we will believe so). However, the "success" of such reforms deflects us from questioning the reasonableness of an economic system that sells poisoned food or hazardous vehicles in the first place.

Conservatives and Liberals may bicker over whether "consumer sovereignty" is best expressed in free or regulated markets, but both are committed to encouraging high levels of essentially irrational consumption. No traditional economist has ever proposed that consumer sovereignty be defined as the rational and coordinated control of production by the users of goods. That of course would lead to the abolition of the capitalist system. However strongly Conservatives and Liberals seem to disagree on the extent of government interference with production, both hold firmly to the principles of maintaining high levels of output as well as the primary goal of production for profit.

THE PERVERSION OF THE SAFETY IDEA

Although the American automobile industry has complained vigorously about the intrusion of the safety experts and the environmentalists and the job-safety people and so on, their argument that regulation is killing the industry is wrong. Insofar as automakers believe their own propaganda along this line of reasoning, they are deceiving themselves. Nevertheless, the auto industry's current stand on auto safety is an instructive episode that reveals much about how the corporate economy operates.

Quite understandably, capitalists want to lower their production costs so that they can improve their profits. Until recently, protectionist intervention in the auto industry scarcely dented profits. Curiously enough, in the past it probably served to increase profits. In 1977, General Motors reported a record-breaking net income of about $4 billion on sales of $55 billion. GM ranked thirty-seventh among all American corporations in net income as a percentage of stockholders' equity. More important, paid earnings per share were two-thirds higher than stockholder earnings a decade earlier, in preconsumerist 1966. Ford and Chrysler also ranked in the top 200 firms in earnings ratio, and their earnings-per-share record was also better than it had been a decade earlier (Ford's had increased almost 100 percent). Not only had manufacturers passed on to consumers all safety costs through monopolistic price setting, but their own profits had continued to rise. They used higher safety costs as a pretext to obtain price increases which represented more than the safety features actually cost. Consumers, warned by the media that auto safety costs money, accepted higher auto prices almost unquestioningly. In fact, no data on actual safety costs are available except what the manufacturers choose to release. The evidence, however, clearly indicates that, whatever the costs, they did not eat into manufacturers' profits until the recent recession took hold.

Despite their public opposition, most American automobile corporations collaborated with the safety people because, initially, one of the corporate benefits of the safety program was to limit foreign competition. The "safe bumper" codes, for instance, promptly eliminated many small foreign makes from American markets or else imposed serious engineering costs that raised their prices. By taking some of the price advantages away from the foreigners, the safety regulations enabled the highly concentrated American automobile industry to increase its monopolistic control over prices, output, and quality.

Ironically, the promise of better and safer cars was thus twisted to produce better profits. And where was the "government of the people" during all this? The answer is simple. While millions have been spent to promote automobile safety, the Justice Department has spent scarcely a penny to investigate price collusion among the car makers. Consumer protection is not to be extended to the pocketbook.

As with all oligopolists, however, there is the tendency to become self-content. Within four years of reporting record-breaking profits, GM and the rest of the industry were running up staggering losses. The retooled Japanese cars were taking an even-larger share of the market as American automakers suddenly found themselves in a competitive market situation. To make matters worse, the whole economy began to slide downward into a deep stagnation after 1979. Cars at any price, safe or unsafe, were out of reach for millions who were out of work or scarcely surviving a grinding inflation. The resulting profit squeeze on the automakers now demanded that costs be cut ruthlessly. Consumer, environmental and job-safety programs, and, finally, their workers' salaries were obvious targets, and the automakers quickly mounted a public-relations and political lobbying effort to "take back" on all these fronts. Once a boon to profit making, auto safety was now depicted as a threat to profits and to the continued strength of a basic American industry. In the new political and economic setting, many consumers even became convinced that we no longer could afford rigorous auto-safety standards.

THE RADICAL DILEMMA

No doubt the Radical position seems hopelessly negativistic and irrelevant to the specific question of "protecting the consumer"; and indeed it is, if Radicals are expected by conventional economists to offer long-run remedies that do not consider the underlying philosophical and social organization of consumption activities in a monopolistic, capitalist society. Before the consistent Radical can take up the automobile-safety question, with all of its elements of deception and unjustified profit making by the auto industry, she or he must ask this question first: Are privately owned automobiles *the* socially desirable form of personal transportation? Liberals and Conservatives, of course, find such a question to be "foolish" and not worthy of serious consideration. Instead, they are content to pretend that what is consumed reflects what consumers truly want. Conservatives adroitly avoid raising the issue of how demand may be manipulated by advertising, and Liberals pay little more than lip service to this problem. Both fail to understand how a "consumer society" may become locked into thoroughly irrational patterns of consumption. However, if we see that most purchases are made simply because the goods are being sold, rather than because we have received cerebral messages that we *need* the particular commodities, it will become easier to unravel the problem of wasteful consumption as well as the consumption of unsafe and dangerous products.

Of course, people shouldn't have to drive unsafe cars, nor should they have to own unsafe "pet rocks" or any other item sold in a capitalist society. Neither should automakers (or even "pet rock" sellers) be able to profit from selling "safe" automobiles (or "safe" pet rocks). For Radicals, however, the point at issue is really whether the goods themselves are socially useful. It is not a matter of making socially wasteful goods "safe." The Radical, then, approaches the question of consumer welfare by questioning the very goods that are offered for sale. In the case of the privately owned automobile and the enormously expensive system of roads and ancillary services needed to make auto ownership feasible, most Radicals see an incredibly irrational and wasteful transportation mode. In fact, Radicals view the recent debate over private automobile safety and the virtual absence of any discussion about devising an efficient system of mass transportation as a good example of how we never address the basic questions in our analysis of consumer behavior.

ISSUE 3

Energy Economics
What Ever Happened to the Energy Crisis?

The fuel industry has been warning . . . for the past decade
that if government regulations continued to keep oil and
natural gas prices too low to generate capital needed to find
oil and gas, our nation would eventually run short.

Gulf Oil Corporation Advertisement, 1973

It's sort of like sex. Everybody's going to get all the gasoline they
need but they're damn sure not going to get all they want.

*R.W. Baldwin, President,
Gulf Refining and Marketing, 1979*

If we have to have people literally freezing to death because
segments of the business community don't think they're enjoying
a sufficient rate of profit—a highly questionable premise in the
oil and gas industry, to say the least—then what is the Federal
Power Commission for?

Congressman John Conyers, 1977

We cannot for the life of us understand why so many liberals in
this country are hostile to business. . . .

Mobil Oil Company, 1977

Left to the mercies of supply and demand, OPEC is finding it can
do nothing more than set its price where the market tells it.

William Tucker, Harper's, 1981

THE PROBLEM

Item: October, 1973 marks the beginning of the energy crisis, as OPEC embargoes crude oil sales to the United States; within a few months the embargo ends but domestic gasoline prices have increased by nearly 100 percent. *Item:* In the frigid winter of 1977, Americans literally run out of available natural gas supplies, schools close, industries and commercial enterprises shut their doors for lack of fuel, and home consumers warily watch their thermostats and anxiously listen for their furnaces. *Item:* In the spring of 1979, the "stable" government of the Shah of Iran collapses into civil war and within a few months the "revolutionary" Khomeini government begins to remove Iran's 10-percent share of world crude production from world markets; in the United States, gasoline shortages again appear at the pump.

The energy crisis had come suddenly and practically without warning. The post-World War II American affluence had created a steady appetite for energy. Americans had bought bigger homes and more and more television sets, electric can openers, and air conditioners. Detroit had built bigger gas-devouring automobiles. On the eve of the 1973 embargo, the annual increase in energy usage was running at a rate of over 4 percent a year, or a little faster than the nation's growth of real GNP. Of particular importance in the surging growth of energy demand was the increased consumer demand for petroleum and natural gas as shown in Table 3.1. Domestic reserves of these two fuels declined quickly through the 1950s and 1960s, and as a result Americans became increasingly dependent upon overseas suppliers to support their energy binge. For a very long time foreign crude oil prices remained extremely low, but there was, of course, no reason to assume that the rest of the world, or at least that part of it that exported energy, would be forever willing to underwrite our gluttony with $2-per-barrel petroleum. Americans, totaling only 5 percent of the world's population, were consuming 35 percent of the world's energy production. Nevertheless, the thought of "running out" of energy was virtually unthinkable. When the Arabs turned off the spigot in 1973, a carefree era came to a sudden and brutal end. Suddenly, and thankfully very briefly, there was no petroleum at any price, and when supplies were available again, crude prices, and thus the prices of gasoline and other fuels, had begun their long and steep climb upward.

Looking back over the past decade of American political and economic history, few events dominated the public interest and controlled

Table 3.1 Distribution of U.S. Energy Consumption

Source	1950	1970
Coal	37.8%	19.1%
Oil	39.5%	43.9%
Natural gas	18.0%	32.7%
Hydro electric	4.7%	4.3%

national policy as did the energy crisis. The fear of running out of oil and natural gas produced important changes in Americans' lifestyles, affecting their work habits, how they built their homes, and what they did with their idle time. Rising energy prices accelerated an already serious inflation problem as heating and energy costs doubled, tripled, and then quadrupled over the decade. Very much as Khomeini's Iran later held American Embassy officials hostage, Americans felt they were held hostage by the OPEC cartel. At the same time, the nation's foreign policy was hostage to our energy needs, requiring that America focus its international efforts in a heretofore largely neglected area of the world. Meanwhile, the greatest redistribution of wealth in the world's history was taking place as hundreds of billions of dollars flowed out of American consumers' pockets and into Middle East nations' treasuries.

By the early 1980s, however, the energy crisis had faded from front-page headlines. Oil, natural gas, and other fuels were still expensive by the old standards and few serious observers maintained that we would ever return to the good old cheap energy days. Yet, by mid 1982 dependency on foreign supplies of petroleum was down to only 20 percent of our consumption, compared to nearly 50 percent before the Arab oil embargo. Although it was certainly only a temporary market condition, there was some talk of an "oil glut" and, indeed gasoline prices fell a bit in 1982. In any case, there was less public and private discussion of "the energy crisis." Even the oil companies and the Arabs, both objects of considerable scorn a decade earlier, hardly attracted much attention.

What had happened? How had the focus of attention changed so quickly? Had the energy crisis indeed been solved? Answers to these questions vary depending on the ideological views of different observers. Even as popular and political concern about an energy crisis declined, debate began to develop over why the problem had ebbed and, more important, whether the diminished sense of crisis was permanent or a purely short-run and therefore deceiving turn of events. The "disappearance" of the energy crisis became about as hot an issue among economists in the early 1980s as the appearance of the crisis had been in the 1970s.

SYNOPSIS. Conservatives maintain that the appearance of the crisis in the 1970s was largely the result of ill-planned government efforts to regulate energy prices and that the current subsiding of the problem is the result of returning to a market-based pricing policy. Liberals see the most recent changes in energy conditions as only temporary and believe that the continuing shortage of energy resources makes it necessary to develop a national energy policy. Radicals, while recognizing the long-run problem of dwindling energy resources, believe the "crisis" was engineered by the energy companies in an effort to "hype" profits.

Anticipating the Arguments

- According to Conservatives, in what specific ways did past government efforts to deal with energy problems contribute to energy shortages? What do Conservatives propose instead?

- On what grounds do Liberals continue to argue for a national energy program?

- On what facts and logic do Radicals base their assertion that the energy crisis has largely been "manipulated?"

The Conservative Argument

From the Conservative point of view, the question as to what happened to the energy crisis is easily answered. It disappeared when the forces of the free market were permitted to establish the pricing and allocation decisions that had been controlled for so long by government intervention. The phasing out of price controls over oil products under President Carter in 1979, the ending of these controls by President Reagan in 1981, and the eventual ending of natural gas price controls will guarantee an end to the crisis atmosphere that pervaded energy questions in the 1970s.

To understand how a free market works, it is perhaps useful to see first how an "unfree" market doesn't work. A brief survey of our past energy policies shows just how intervention in the market to "protect" the nation instead does it serious harm.

THE ROOTS OF THE ENERGY PROBLEM

Until the 1960s, Americans enjoyed a false sense of security—perhaps it was simple ignorance—about energy matters. With abundant supplies of petroleum, coal, and natural gas within the continental United States, Americans had come to believe they were energy independent. They were, for a while. Even when American petroleum production failed to quench our gasoline thirst, we found it easy to believe that all that Middle Eastern oil was there for our taking. At 19¢ a gallon at the pump (plus a free set of dishes for a full tank), the American owner of a two-ton gas-guzzling "Torpedo 8" had few energy concerns. What, after all, was there to worry about?

A closer look, however, would have shown the growing vulnerability of the American position. First of all, the incredible American appetite for energy could not be offset forever by a steady flood of inexpensive new supplies. Second, and most important, the American government was following policies that sooner or later would lead to market failure. As a result, American consumers were becoming dangerously dependent upon a supply situation over which American oil retailers had little control.

The crisis began quietly enough in 1960 when the Organization of Oil Exporting Countries (OPEC) was founded. At the time, the event was little noted, and OPEC seemed an ineffective "debating society," with each of the exporting nations struggling unsuccessfully to advance its own particular interests. This approach soon would change as events in the United States gave the "debating society" the power of an effective cartel. As we increased our petroleum consumption and our dependence on imported oil, *we* actually created the OPEC cartel. Coal, with which America was well endowed, was losing favor among industrial and home consumers, who preferred cleaner and more adaptable petroleum. However, this trend was accelerated greatly by government actions. The environmentalists' Clean Air Act of 1970 placed serious legal restrictions on the continued industrial use of coal, artificially increasing the demand for oil. Natural gas, meanwhile, was being "costed out of the market" as the Federal Power Commission, which had regulated natural-gas prices since 1938, followed a policy of keeping natural gas prices close to production costs. With profits virtually eliminated in natural-gas production, there was little incentive to drill for new gas, and the ratio of proved reserves to annual production fell from 27 to 1 in 1950 to 13 to 1 by 1970.

Because of the declining demand for some alternative energy sources and the dwindling supply of others, along with the growing gluttony of American consumers, the U.S. demand for oil grew enormously—from 10.23 million barrels per day in 1962 to 15.98 million barrels per day in 1972. The growth in demand for oil, however, did not lead to expanded U.S. production, as would be expected in a normal market situation. The trouble was that, like natural gas, there was no normal market for domestic oil. Rising oil demand did exert upward pressures on domestic oil prices at first, and drillers sought new petroleum sources in Alaska and at offshore sites. After the much publicized Santa Barbara blowout in 1969, the environmentalists succeeded in ending all offshore drilling. Under environmental pressures, the Alaska Pipeline construction moved along slowly and expensively. Domestic oil supplies were not growing to meet demand, so, as the laws of supply and demand would have it, prices were forced upward. However, as oil prices (along with other prices in the economy) edged upward in late 1971, the government slapped price controls on domestic oil production.

As Figure 3.1 indicates, U.S. production peaked in 1970, but consumption continued to grow. The difference, of course, was made up by imported oil. At first the dangers were not noticed. At $2 per barrel, Saudi crude seemed a good deal for everyone—oil companies, U.S. business, and ordinary consumers. By 1973, about 40 percent of our oil was coming from abroad (in 1954, we had imported only 8 percent). Practically no one seemed to realize that our increased dependence left us open to cartel action by our suppliers. When the OPEC ministers walked out on negotiations with oil companies in October 1973, American newspapers failed to cover the story. The Arab-Israeli war a few months later proved the proper pretext for the OPEC cartel to assert its existence. Oil shipments by OPEC members to the U.S. ceased and the energy crisis began.

THE FAILURE TO DEVELOP AN ENERGY POLICY

Within a year, Saudi crude went from $2.60 per barrel to $11.65. The price seemed outrageous, but ill-planned U.S. Government policies actually made prices rise further during the next seven years—to

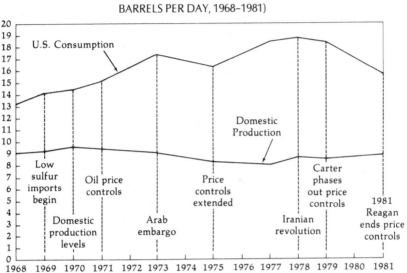

FIGURE 3.1   HOW PRICE CONTROLS CREATED THE ENERGY CRISIS
(AVERAGE CONSUMPTION OF OIL IN U.S. IN MILLIONS OF
BARRELS PER DAY, 1968–1981)

Source: U.S. Bureau of the Census, *Export and Import Trade Statistics*, 1981.

over $40 per barrel by 1980. Rather than freeing up domestic produc-
tion, which certainly would have been stimulated by the pricing strategy of OPEC, we followed the same old head-in-the-sand policies of
the past. President Ford's 1975 call to put a $2 tax on foreign oil and
end oil price controls was rejected by a Liberal Congress. The Liberals
argued that these actions would only raise gasoline and home heating
oil prices and produce enormous profits for American oil companies.
In the short run, they were right, but in the long run such a program
would have (1) reduced U.S. consumption by placing even higher
prices on overseas oil, (2) encouraged U.S. oil discovery and development, (3) stimulated development and use of other energy sources,
and, most important, (4) reestablished a free market in which energy
prices would reflect real supply-and-demand conditions.

Following the Liberal policy simply perpetuated the power of the
OPEC cartel. With price controls on domestic production extended in
1975, we became more dependent on foreign crude. Moreover, Americans quickly adapted to the higher fuel and gasoline prices and, after a

brief decline in consumption, returned to the old bad habits. By the winter of 1977, consumption was about 19 million barrels a day. With consumption 15 percent greater than it had been in 1971, when the price was 10 percent lower, many Arab sheiks rubbed their hands gleefully over the apparently inelastic American demand for petroleum.

Had it not been for two unrelated events in 1977 and 1978, it is hard to predict how much longer Americans would have continued to make vast transfers of their wealth to the OPEC cartel. First came the cruelty of a bitterly cold winter; second the Ayatollah Khomeini.

A NEW POLICY EMERGES

This time, however, reason began to prevail. In late 1980, President Carter grudgingly announced that price controls over domestic oil production would be phased out. This was a clear admission that government maintenance of low energy prices was the major cause of any energy shortage. With President Reagan's ending of all controls in 1981, the way was clear to returning to market-determined pricing and production of petroleum. Only decontrol over natural gas (promised in 1985) remained to be accomplished.

The effect of the change in energy policy only now is being felt; however, the right things are happening. With the lid off domestic prices, domestic production has stopped declining and actually is beginning to rise. In the last six months of 1981, drilling for new domestic oil increased by 50 percent. Consumption of OPEC oil is less than half what it was during the cartel's heyday; moreover, with a competitive condition reestablished in U.S. energy markets, OPEC's pricing power is fast waning. At the same time, American consumers finally are learning the "conservation" that the market teaches. Unprotected by a Congress that would repeal the laws of supply and demand, higher energy prices are reducing the old American appetite for energy. Also, higher prices induce the private development of cheaper energy sources, thus increasing our energy independence over the long run.

Compared to what Americans have been used to, the Conservative solution *does* cost more, although probably not so much as is generally believed. The relative price of energy-consuming goods must rise. This will necessitate consumer reshuffling of choices and changed consumption patterns; however, since nothing is free, it is the only possible solution this side of the Kingdom of Oz. Liberals and Radicals may dress up their panaceas by creating impressive regulatory agencies or by calling for national-resource and economic planning, but they cannot avoid the reality of higher-priced goods. This can be the only logical outcome to the energy crisis. And the Conservative solution still relies on the market and advocates individual freedom.

The Liberal Argument

As of this writing, the Conservatives are right in one of their generalizations. The public concern over the energy crisis has ebbed. They are wrong, however, when they argue that the crisis has gone away, and they are doubly wrong when they maintain that the free-market determination of energy prices is our only assurance of a trouble-free future. On the contrary, the unrestrained emphasis on corporate profit making that caused the energy crisis in 1973 and 1977, and again in 1979, promises only disaster in the future.

THE FALLACIES OF THE CONSERVATIVE ARGUMENT

Before proceeding, it is necessary to clear up a few energy "facts" introduced by the Conservative argument. First, U.S. energy usage indeed has gone down since President Carter began to phase out price controls in 1979. Conservatives maintain that this is the result of higher, market-determined prices compelling Americans to economize in their energy use. To them, this is proof that the market makes the best and most intelligent resource allocations. The argument, however, exhibits the logical fallacy of misplaced emphasis. Sure, there has been some reduced usage as a result of controls being lifted and prices taking off, but the cruel fact of the old and the poor shivering in dark and cold rooms is scarcely humane proof that the market works. Nevertheless, most of the recent energy conservation is neither the result of rising prices nor the "reasonableness" of the market. The primary cause is that the economy has been in a long period of recession and stagnation since 1979. An economy with 9 to 10 percent unemployment rates and with such basic industries as construction, steel, and autos all but shut down certainly doesn't consume the energy of a booming economy. Quite simply, evidence suggests that energy usage correlates much more directly with economic activity than with energy price changes. This was the experience of the 1975–1979 period when, in a booming economy, consumers were willing to pay outrageous OPEC prices. Unless Conservatives also want to take responsibility for the recent depressed condition of the economy—a "Reagan recession" for instance—they cannot claim responsibility for our recent energy conservation.

A second Conservative argument is that rising fuel-oil and natural-gas prices actually will increase the nation's supply of energy in the long run. According to their view, with rising energy prices, new domestic sources of conventional fuels will be found, old sources (such as coal and nuclear power) will become economically feasible, and new synthetic fuels will be developed—the best of all possible worlds. Again, the evidence does not support the analysis. It fails to recognize that the oil companies *control* most of these energy sources. Over the past decade, largely with profits gathered during the years of the oil crisis, Exxon, Mobil, and the other giants have added control of vast amounts of coal, shale oil, natural gas, and uranium deposits to their domestic oil holdings. Given their market position, these same companies control practically all synthetic-fuel development. The point is that with control over alternative energy sources, there is very little economic reason to develop them, especially if prices of oil and natural gas remain high. The record supports this conclusion, for, after oil prices were decontrolled and natural gas began its gradual decontrol, most of the so-called energy companies shelved their development plans for alternative fuels. While such alternative energy sources eventually may be employed, they will not be developed as long as high-priced oil and gas are still available and still can be sold. We have not moved any closer to energy abundance.

A third point that Conservatives gloss over is the question of energy independence. While it is true that the share of foreign oil we consume has declined from nearly 50 percent of our total consumption at the time of the 1973 Arab embargo to less than 30 percent, a short-term trend should not be cited simply to confuse the facts. The point to remember is that we are still dangerously dependent upon unstable national governments and uncertain political conditions for our own economic well-being.

THE FAILURE OF THE MARKET TO WORK IN THE PAST

While Conservatives argue that a national energy policy can be determined best by simple reliance on the market mechanism, there is quite enough evidence to dispute the point. We cannot expect any corporation to consider the long-run social planning required for a workable energy program. The nature of the market is to maximize profits in the comparatively short run, not to balance long-run social costs and benefits. Thus, any program aimed at resolving the energy crisis must emanate from the federal government, where the power of law and the inducements of taxes and subsidies can direct the private sector toward desired objectives.

Proof that corporate decision making is aimed at maximizing profits rather than social benefit is abundant as more information is obtained on the oil embargo and crisis of 1973. While Americans waited in line for a few gallons of high-priced gasoline, corporate balance sheets showed no signs of distress. Precisely as the OPEC nations were supposedly putting the squeeze on the oil companies in 1972 and 1973, after-tax profits for the nine largest oil producers averaged a whopping 45-percent increase. For Exxon and Gulf, the profit increase was 60 percent. Additional evidence from several government reports now shows that the real scarcity of oil and gasoline was not nearly so great as the corporations maintained. Although there was a scarcity of certain fuel types in certain regions, this was largely the result of bad business decision making. Moreover, many companies actually had been cutting back overseas production before 1973 in an attempt to raise prices by reducing supplies. Even during the height of the shortage hysteria, as fuel prices edged upward daily, some oil importers reported shortfalls when they actually had sufficient supplies on hand. The effect, of course, was to kick prices and profits up even more. With such a record, it would be unsound to rely on corporate wisdom to solve the energy problem in a socially desirable way.

THE LOST INITIATIVE

By the late 1970s, the evidence was clear for those who cared to see it: The United States needed a firm and effective federally administered energy policy. Reliance upon purely private solutions could not assure that the whole nation would receive the energy that was essential in amounts and at rates that did not create regional economic dislocations. Moreover, a federal policy, besides maintaining equity, would be the only way to deal with problems posed by OPEC's price rulings and with the "profits first" bias of American Energy companies. Experience showed us that the days of depending upon the market laws of supply and demand were over. Supply-and-demand controls were too important to be left to the market to resolve.

For a fleeting moment it appeared that we finally might develop a comprehensive energy program. In October 1978, Jimmy Carter's energy bill passed both houses of Congress with great fanfare. The legislation, however, was simply inadequate for the task. It did provide taxes on gas-guzzling automobiles and subsidies to homeowners and industries who converted to solar heat. Tax credits were given to public utilities that converted to coal. On the negative side, however, the bill laid the groundwork for decontrolling natural gas and, therefore, for pumping enormous profits into the coffers of the energy giants.

Liberals' doubts about the fairness and effectiveness of the Carter approach to the energy problem were heightened in mid 1979 when the President announced his decision to permit price decontrol of "old" domestic crude oil over the next two years. According to Carter, this would increase U.S. output and reduce the effectiveness of the OPEC cartel. Few Liberals were convinced. What it would do, most believed, would be to provide enormous profits for the oil companies as they raised prices of domestic crude to the going OPEC price. The President's proposal for a moderate "windfall" profits tax on these earnings did not make his action more palatable. Any windfall to the oil companies could only swell their bloated profits, thus diminishing their interest in developing cheaper oil substitutes.

The political moment for developing a usable national energy policy had been lost. The final blow came with the presidential victory of Ronald Reagan two years later. Reagan's goals were clear, as he moved to dismantle the Department of Energy created by Carter, and accelerated the price decontrol process. We had returned to the old policy of no policy at all.

THE CONTINUING NEED FOR AN ENERGY POLICY

The nation still remains hostage to OPEC and to the energy companies. No program exists for allocating energy supplies fairly except through the indifferent forces of the market. Plans to ration energy, to conserve energy, and to develop alternative sources—all problems pointed out in the past energy crises—have been shelved. The possible catastrophe of such a situation is not widely recognized; yet, despite the temporary ebbing of an immediate energy crisis, we nevertheless will face another crisis in the future. The supply of the world's energy sources is limited, but energy demand is not. This simple fact requires that we develop a comprehensive energy plan.

Such an overall energy policy must be aimed at (1) ending American dependence on foreign energy sources, (2) encouraging the development of alternative energy fuels, (3) developing programs that lead to lowered energy demand, and (4) fairly allocating and pricing energy fuels among all sectors of the economy. Since none of these objectives are likely to be obtained under present conditions, direct government intervention in the energy market is required.

Basically, two alternative approaches are possible. Both are consistent with a free-enterprise economy but still offer the added benefit of public planning and control.

Under the first alternative, the production, distribution, and pricing of most energy fuels could be regulated tightly. That is, a public energy regulatory agency could oversee all of these operations, making sure national objectives were reached. Production targets, output allocation, production reserves, and alternative fuel development could be set by commission decisions. Excessive profits could be controlled by establishing and maintaining "fair returns" profit targets for the controlled companies.

Under the second alternative, which should be attractive to "true Conservatives," a competitive market situation could be established in the energy field, breaking up the collusive pricing and production practices of the present giants. Not only could the big energy companies be broken up into smaller units, but they could be required to divest themselves of certain operations. After choosing which of the production, refining, and marketing operations they cared to remain in, the companies would have to sell off their other holdings. This would effectively end the wellhead-to-pump control they now maintain. In such a competitive situation, the use of tax-subsidy mixes would be effective in directing or encouraging business actions to meet national energy objectives.

There are arguments for and against both of these approaches to implementing an energy program; however, either one is more attractive than the course we are following presently. Economic theory and the events of the past decade show that a tightly controlled energy cartel will act only to maximumize total profits with little regard for social needs. The failed record of corporate responsibility in the past makes public energy control essential.

The Radical Argument

Although Americans have become generally inclined to blame the OPEC cartel and Arab nationalism in particular for higher energy prices, it is increasingly evident that American energy companies were the prime movers in creating the initial panic over fuel shortfalls. Moreover, they have benefited handsomely as a result.

A MANIPULATED CRISIS

In the early 1970s American oil company earnings had leveled off. Even under tax arrangements with the federal government—which allowed the oil producers to deduct all OPEC established price increases at the wellhead from their domestic taxes—after-tax profits in 1972 were just about the same as they had been four years earlier. Meanwhile, the pesky environmentalists, after the Santa Barbara oil spill, had succeeded in stalling industry plans for the Alaska Pipeline, additional offshore drilling, and new refinery and super-tanker port facilities. Fuel consumption in the United States was going up, but not fast enough by itself to produce a drastic price increase. Thus, when the Arab embargo was announced in the winter of 1973–1974, the oil companies greeted it as a blessing.

All during the winter and during most of 1974, Americans teetered between concern and panic as they queued up at gas stations to get a few dollars' worth of gasoline. The oil companies flooded the media with "save fuel" commercials that darkly alluded to no more cars, or no more jobs, or no heat in the house. Meanwhile, the government laid plans for full-fledged gasoline rationing. Americans had come face-to-face with an "energy crisis."

A constant theme in the corporate campaigns was that the crisis was the people's fault. (By and large, Americans themselves blamed the Arabs, but it would have been tactless for the oil importing companies to point the finger at their suppliers.) Americans were told that they were energy gluttons. In point of fact they were, but not as a matter of individual choice. Without any thought to an eventual energy crisis, Americans had been sold almost every energy-wasting commodity possible. Indeed, during the peak of the "energy crisis," thoughtful television viewers must have noted some irony in a situation that juxtaposed an earnest electric company commercial instructing viewers on how to cut down on electricity and snappy jingles pushing air conditioners and other appliances.

The oil embargo and the following "energy crisis" education campaign quickly brought benefits to the oil companies. Prices of oil products went up and up, with presidential and congressional blessings. Environmentalists, some of whom may have been initially ambivalent on how to handle the energy question, were driven to the wall by the nearly universal demand to exploit new oil and other energy sources. The issue came to be understood as a choice between ecology and jobs. Meanwhile, oil price increases soon drove up the price of all fuels, and oil companies such as Exxon began referring to themselves as "energy companies," proudly reporting their growing interests in coal, nuclear energy, and even solar power.

After three years, the list of corporate gains from the energy crisis seemed limitless. Prices were up. Profits were up. Vertical integration from wellhead to gas pump had increased. The American and world market percentages of the top nine oil giants had grown. Substitute energy sources had gone up in price, and the leading oil producers were quietly gaining control of these industries. Natural gas prices, although still controlled, were also raised slightly (though not enough to suit the oil companies). The government was pledging tax advantages and subsidies to companies willing to undertake energy research. And all that silly talk about environmental priorities had been shelved.

The blunt fact is that there never was a real energy shortage. As subsequent inquiries showed, oil companies held back supplies and hid available oil at sea in tankers during the crisis of 1973–1974. When the prices of gasoline and fuel oil went up, oil suddenly and mysteriously became available. The inexorable search for profits, not Mideastern politics, had been the basis of the oil shortage.

Consumption of energy in the United States did fall slightly (by about 6 percent) between 1973 and 1975. The decline, however, cannot be credited entirely to the energy crisis. In fact if we take into account the full-fledged recession of those years, it is possible that the savings had nothing to do with conscious reduction in consumption. By 1977, at any rate, energy consumption was well above 1973 levels. Even with additional OPEC price increases, the oil giants cheerfully increased the flow of foreign oil, and American crude production sagged.

What the Arabs had been in 1973 to the oil companies, "the winter of '77" was to the natural gas combines. (It should be mentioned that most of the natural-gas supply had by now fallen under the control of the oil giants; the energy program of the oil companies, after the earlier crisis, had aimed at developing a broad monopolistic control over virtually all energy sources.) As the bitter months of January and February passed, Americans were told that they were running out of gas supplies. Schools and factories closed, and, at President Carter's request, consumers turned their thermostats down to 65° Fahrenheit and lower. Congress, meanwhile, rushed through emergency energy legislation that laid the basis for natural-gas decontrol. Charges of industry manipulation were ignored as the freeze grew more severe. There was of course no real shortage, only a short supply of what would be marketed at the existing regulated price. The object of the industry-created scarcity was to end controls and force the price upward. Just as there was no gasoline shortage at $1.50 per gallon, there would be no natural-gas shortage if rates doubled. Meanwhile, the crisis managers again talked the American people into believing the higher prices were the natural, if unpleasant, result of the laws of supply and demand.

In mid 1979, gasoline shortages reappeared. Using the pretext of shortfalls supposedly resulting from the Iranian revolution and OPEC's reluctance to sell, the oil companies prepared a new assault on consumers. With the appearance of gas lines, and encouraged by the Carter administration's helpful statements that matters were bound to get worse, the oil companies sought again to create the crisis atmosphere that would justify a new round of permanent price increases. However, none of the oil companies could quite explain the supposed shortfalls in light of available evidence that showed crude imports rising and gasoline refineries working at near capacity.

NATIONALIZE, DON'T SUBSIDIZE

The appearance of gasoline gluts and falling profits for energy corporations in the early 1980s has recently produced confusion about the energy problem. Cheered on by Conservatives, who claim that the "forces of the market" have solved the energy crisis, many Americans may falsely believe that the era of escalating energy prices is over. In fact, it has only temporarily been washed away by economic hard times. Worldwide economic recession has reduced the power of the energy giants to contrive the crisis atmosphere essential for enormous price increases.

These lessons should not be misunderstood. As ecologists can point out, there is indeed a real energy crisis waiting out there in the future. There may even be short-term crises in the near future as a result of further OPEC pricing actions. Thus there is a need for an energy policy—one that explores environmentally safe energy alternatives and one that attempts to deal with America's massive energy waste and disproportionate use of the world's energy supply.

The first step in developing such a program must be the elimination of production-for-profit objectives in the energy field. The lessons of the past ten years should show that an energy policy dominated by a few monopolistic oil companies, with the government as their accomplice and agent, is not an energy strategy but a profit strategy. At a minimum, then, the beginning of an energy policy is the nationalization of energy resources. Regulation, tax-subsidy policies, and jawboning have never worked to control the energy industries. Attempts to end monopoly abuse through breaking up the oil companies is without any special economic benefit and is probably politically more difficult than sweeping nationalization.

Energy resources—their intelligent development and fair distribution—are everyone's problem, not the special province of a few enterprises interested in profit maximization. These resources are too important to be left to the whims of capitalist control. Moreover, national control and the rational use of energy resources is also a first requirement in inaugurating an effective environmental policy. With private ownership of energy resources and under the threat of constant energy shortages, ecological concern will always be traded off for greater profits. Thus, a Radical energy program requires that energy be considered a national resource problem. The use, pricing, and distribution of this resource should be handled by a nonpartisan agency acting in behalf of people's, not corporate, interest.

Monopoly Power

What Should Be Our Policy toward Big Business?

People of the same trade seldom meet together, even for merriment and diversion, but the conversation ends in a conspiracy against the public, or in some contrivance to raise prices.

Adam Smith, 1776

Every contract, combination in the form of trust or otherwise, or conspiracy, in restraint of trade or commerce . . . is hereby declared to be illegal. . . . Every person who shall monopolize, or attempt to monopolize, or combine or conspire . . . to monopolize . . . shall be deemed guilty of a misdemeanor.

Sherman Anti-Trust Act, 1890

The problem in America is not that the top 100 corporation presidents are violating the laws, though God knows they are; the problem is they're writing the laws.

Nicholas Johnson,
Federal Communications Commissioner, 1972

THE PROBLEM

A paradoxical situation appears when we examine the structure and organization of American business enterprise. On the one hand, the official ideology of American capitalism espouses competition and we have created legal and administrative arrangements to maintain competition. But there is wide disagreement as to whether modern corporate size and integration represent a monopoly threat to the economic and social organization of society. Technically speaking, "literal monopoly" in the United States is quite rare. According to the textbook definition of monopoly, a monopolist is the sole producer of a commodity that has no close substitutes. As "price makers," the textbooks tell us, monopolies must be regulated. The classic example usually cited is one of the public utilities.

The current debate over monopoly power, however, is not really about public utilities. Rather, it is about the monopolistic power of companies that are not literal monopolists. It is about the current tendency toward merger and combination of American business enterprises and what this tendency portends.

Since the passage of the Sherman Anti-Trust Act in 1890, a considerable body of law has been enacted "to protect competition." The essence of these accumulated laws may be summarized as follows.

1. It is illegal to enter into a contract, combination, or conspiracy in restraint of trade; or to monopolize, attempt to monopolize, or to combine or conspire to monopolize trade.

2. When the effect is to lessen competition or create a monopoly, it is illegal to acquire the stock or assets of competing companies, to discriminate among purchasers other than what can be justified by actual costs, or to enter into exclusive or tying contracts.

3. Under all cases, whether the effect is to monopolize or not, it is illegal to serve in the directorships of competing corporations, to use unfair methods of competition, or to employ unfair or deceptive acts or practices.

Despite the thrust of theory and law, however, few observers of American capitalism would deny the existence of big business. Moreover, many would argue that antitrust law has had little effect in slowing the tendency toward bigness. As Figure 4.1 illustrates, the merger activity of the past fifteen or twenty years has been considerable, easily dwarfing the more well-known merger periods of the 1890s (the era of the trust) and

FIGURE 4.1   NUMBERS OF MAJOR MERGERS AND ACQUISITIONS, 1895–1980

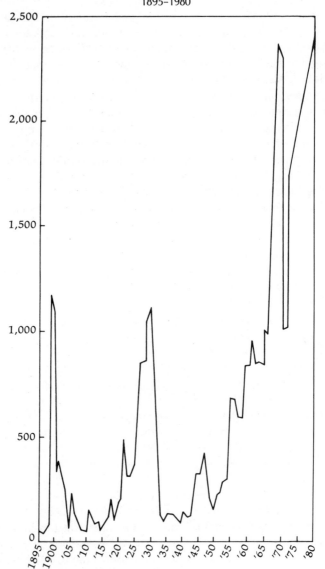

the 1920s (the era of the holding company). The obvious effect of such consolidation activity has been to concentrate more and more of the nation's productive capacity into fewer corporations. For instance, in 1945 the nation's 200 largest manufacturing firms owned 45 percent of all assets of U.S. industry. Today they own over 60 percent. Looking at the data somewhat differently, we find that 94 percent of all U.S. corporate assets are owned by just 12 percent of the nation's corporations.

What is the significance of this growing business concentration? To what extent are large firms able to act as "price makers," setting excessive prices, restricting output, and creating market inefficiency? To what degree do antitrust law, foreign competition, and other economic developments offset or negate the trend toward bigness?

While no economist, regardless of ideological preference, denies the existence of big business, there is widespread disagreement as to whether modern corporate size and integration represents a serious monopoly threat to the economic and social organization of American society.

SYNOPSIS. The Conservative argument asserts that there are sufficient market and legal checks to make certain that big business does not act in an exploitative way but actually improves our economic well-being. The Liberal argument accepts the fact of "bigness" but maintains that government intervention is essential to control potential monopoly exploitation. The Radical argument holds that monopoly is the logical historical development of capitalism and that there is no way to halt this tendency without abolishing the production-for-profit system.

Anticipating the Arguments

- How do Conservatives argue that bigness in business is not proof of growing monopolistic power?

- What role do Liberals propose for government in dealing with the rise of giant enterprise, and how does their view differ from the Conservative approach?

- How do Radicals support their claim that the growth of alleged monopolistic business behavior in the United States is "merely the logical progression of capitalist development?"

The Conservative Argument

Public discussion of the so-called "monopoly problem" in the United States usually is characterized by gross misunderstandings. Foremost among these is the confusion of bigness with monopoly, and the resulting corollary that big is bad. The anti-big-business attitude that emerges from these views is a serious threat to the American economic system. Far from leading to the rebirth of a competitive business society, most antimonopoly efforts erode free enterprise itself. Ironically, an attack on big business boils down to an attack on business of all kinds. More than they realize, the owners of mom-and-pop grocery stores and the like are themselves threatened by assaults on A&P, IBM, GM, and other business giants.

BIGNESS DOES NOT EQUAL MONOPOLY

Bigness in and of itself is not proof of monopoly power. Of course, there is no denying that concentration of markets and capital exists among manufacturing industries, but concentration does not necessarily mean collusion or domination. The share of the market held by the four auto producers ranges from General Motors' more than 50 percent to American Motors' 4 percent. Yet, as any car buyer knows, competition exists. This is readily apparent in competing advertising, warranties, and styling—as well as in the customary habit of haggling with any car salesperson. Moreover, there are many cases of interindustry competition among different "concentrated" industries. For instance, glass, aluminum, steel, paper, and plastic all battle each other for the food-container market. Nor should international competition be forgotten. While tariffs and shipping costs do offer some protection to American firms, the protection is not absolute—witness the 10- to 20-percent share of the auto market seized by foreign car makers. The point is simple. Big business, far from ending competition, has in fact heightened it. The solitary village blacksmith, barrel maker, or flour miller of a century ago had a far greater monopoly power over price, quality, and output than does his present-day business counterpart.

Those who worry about excessive monopoly power should consider one further point. In a market society, the great check against price gouging, by GM or by a barrel maker, is consumer demand. If prices go too high, sellers simply cannot sell their products—or enough of them to make a profit—and prices will be reduced.

If we can get beyond the silly but appealing logic of the "big is bad" argument, we might actually understand that the opposite is much more nearly correct: Big business has been good for America.

Big business has been the major vehicle of economic and technical advance in the United States. (It has done so much that people even believe totally nonsensical rumors about it—for example, that Exxon, or some other oil giant, purchased and buried the patent for an engine that gets fifty miles to a gallon of gas.) Few can deny that product progress and relatively falling prices for most consumer and producer goods during the twentieth century have been the result of expensive technological advancements; these could have resulted only from the great capital concentration and large-scale marketing strategies of big enterprise. Would those who want to abolish GM also want to abolish the assembly-line production technique with its efficiency and savings?

Recently, Liberal and Radical critics of business enterprise have directed their wrath against so-called "conglomerate mergers," combinations of companies in different lines of business. Such attacks are threats to business growth, since conglomerate mergers presently account for about 90 percent of all combinations. This strategy is an extension of the "big is bad" argument; however, it fails to consider that conglomerate mergers also may provide consumer benefits. By strengthening inefficient and costly businesses through improved management techniques and by providing badly needed capital, prices will be lowered. Moreover, the conglomerate merger actually increases competition by resuscitating firms that otherwise would fail.

In any case, bigness is vastly overemphasized. Of America's 11 million businesses, 10.8 million qualify as small businesses according to the Small Business Administration. Regardless of the size of the giant enterprises, no other economy can boast the proportion of small, independent enterprises to the entire population. Small business employs more than 60 percent of the total workforce. Meanwhile, the smallest of the small, those employing twenty or fewer workers, are the fastest growing segment of the business economy, hiring two out of every three current entrants into the labor market. Given these characteristics of American business enterprise, it becomes obvious that big business, even if it were a problem, gets undue attention from Liberals and Radicals. Smallness and competition remain the dominant characteristic of American enterprise.

Singling out big business is unfair and misleading. Even if business bigness were demonstrably bad, why isn't the same logic applied to big government or big labor unions? Those who cry monopoly in the business sector rarely apply that argument against the United Auto Workers or the Teamsters, nor do they see the bureaucratic state management of pricing—from hospital rooms to gasoline stations—as analogous to the imagined monopoly power of big enterprise.

GOVERNMENT CREATES MONOPOLY POWER

This discussion of the bigness issue is not meant to dodge the fact that literal monopoly does sometimes exist, but most such monopolies may be defended on technical grounds. Competing telephone companies would plainly cause a communications nightmare. This type of public utility monopoly, for the most part, is rigorously regulated. As might be expected, such regulation scarcely ever "improves" the monopoly, since profit and pricing goals are subordinated to irrational regulation decisions (see Issue 5 on the railroads). Even when technical monopolies exist, it is still preferable to allow business freedom than to impose inefficient regulation. Other government actions, such as preferential tariffs and tax legislation, also tend to generate inefficient monopoly situations, with the consumer as the ultimate loser. Government intervention is very largely responsible for whatever monopolistic inefficiency exists in the United States today.

Government, of course, is not the sole source of monopoly abuse. As Adam Smith suggested, "They *do* talk business at the country club." Still, while efforts at private cartelization and price conspiracy do occur, they have rarely worked—partly because of greed and partly because of our antitrust laws, which affirm the common-law doctrine that "combinations in restraint of trade" are illegal. Clearly, any truly collusive effort to rig the market must be opposed. In other words, the only rational antimonopoly policy is an anticonspiracy policy; this means ending collusion not just among business people whose greed outstrips their inventiveness, but also that encouraged by government among labor unions.

In the past, government antitrust policy often has wavered on defining monopoly policy. Frequently actions were initiated against firms purely on the grounds that they were big or that they were too profitable. Such an approach works against the development of dynamic and thriving firms. It is rather like punishing the winning runner in a race because he ran too fast. The profitable business is not the only loser, however; so is the society that has benefited in jobs and lower product prices from the large firm's efficiency. Recently, however, two landmark antitrust cases seem to be restoring some reason to our public policy toward big business.

THE PROMISE OF A NEW APPROACH

In the 1982 dismissal of a government action against IBM for monopolizing the mainframe computer industry, the Justice Department agreed that, despite IBM's size and its share of the market, there was no proof that the firm had acted monopolistically. The decision should stand as an important legal landmark against those who would penalize a firm thoughtlessly simply because it has been successful. Meanwhile, in the AT&T case, decided at the same time as the IBM decision, the Justice Department affirmed the doctrine of competition. In this case, AT&T's monopoly power in the buying and selling of communications equipment and services was ended. AT&T was proven guilty of using its power (provided by government as a regulated monopoly) to exclude competitors from the data and electronic transmission market. AT&T was compelled to divest itself of its purely "public utility" local phone operations and join battle fairly with the other "big boys" (including IBM) in the information systems market. For the forseeable future, a useful antitrust policy is in place: *Bigness itself does not prove collusion or unfair price setting but when such activities are proved they will be halted.*

Conservatives must not deny the existence of monopoly when it is real. Very clearly, monopoly power is unjustifiable and injurious to individuals. It prevents efficient allocation of resources. However, aside from those cases of monopoly initiated or encouraged by the government and occasional conspiratorial endeavors by individual enterprises (and even here government tax or purchase policies often stimulate criminal activity), the "monopoly problem" is mostly a phony issue. Liberals use it as a pretext for urging massive social or governmental interference with the market, while Radicals find it convenient as an excuse for their revolutionary assault on the entire system. Both groups would use the issue in a self-serving fashion to extinguish individualism and private property rights.

The Liberal Argument

Traditional economic analysis since Adam Smith has argued that the "great regulator" for business activity is the market. Here, small, competitive firms struggle against each other to sell goods and gain customers. The prices and the possibility of exploitation are always regulated by the "invisible hand" of supply and demand. While we may nit-pick over whether this type of pure competition ever existed outside of economists' minds, it certainly does not exist in the United States today. Just 2,000 businesses in all fields of the economy produce about half of our GNP; the "invisible hand" has largely been replaced by the highly visible fist of corporate power.

THE PROBLEM OF POLICY SELECTION

While most modern-day Conservatives tend to equivocate on the issue of big business, preferring not to see any monopoly problems except in the rarest of cases or only in cases where government "interferes" with the market, Liberals face the problem directly. *Business concentration does exist in the United States.* The policy issue, then, is not a matter of recognizing the obvious but of determining how to deal with it.

The most rudimentary analysis of monopoly behavior tells us that, all things being equal, monopolistic firms tend to charge higher prices and produce less than otherwise might be expected under competitive conditions. They employ fewer workers at lower wages and generally foster resource misallocation. Moreover, the greater the degree of monopoly power, the greater the consumer exploitation.

The implications of this line of economic analysis are clear. The return of competition is apparently the only way to return to economic virtue. In a policy sense, this must mean the enforcement of a vigorous antimonopoly policy, leading to the restructuring of industry into greater numbers of similar-sized units of production. Liberals are not in total agreement on this point, but most would oppose a grand "dividing up" of giant enterprises. First of all, the practical ap-

plication of a literal "break-them-up" policy is not politically or legally feasible. We long ago passed the point of being able to return to
some romantic eighteenth-century concept of the marketplace. This is
not to say that stimulation of competition in certain industries might
not be desirable or possible through the application of antitrust laws.
In fact, the Justice Department must always be prepared to initiate
antimonopoly legal action, but this could not be carried out on a
broad scale without weakening our legal and economic structures.
Second, there is no solid evidence that pure competition would be
beneficial, even if it could be attained without seriously wrenching the
society.

What these observations mean in a practical context is that concentration in the oil industry might be approached differently from
concentration in the auto industry. Domestic automobile production
is limited to just four firms, with General Motors alone producing between 50 and 60 percent of the output. Charges that GM works effectively as a price leader are difficult to question. However, price leadership does not necessarily mean consumer exploitation. Nor would
breaking up GM necessarily lead to social improvement. Even though
GM's size probably has pushed it well beyond what is necessary for at-
taining efficiency from economies of scale, there is no assurance that
forty or even a dozen smaller GMs could produce a product of similar
price and quality and hire the workforce that the present monster
does. On the other hand, information recently released by the Department of Energy indicated that the oil industry, with less actual concentration, conspired during recent energy crises to force up the prices of
gasoline and natural gas by withholding supplies.

The point is that there are different types of giant enterprises—
some highly predatory and exploitative and others reasonably responsible to the public interest. Size alone is no justification for "breaking
up" the auto industry. But the behavior of the oil industry is the worst
kind of monopolistic activity. There are no easy "monopoly tests."
Each case must be taken on its own merits.

Having rejected the rigid competitive argument, we are left to accept the reality of modern corporate concentration. However, though
Liberals realize that bigness itself need not be proof of monopoly
abuse, they do not subscribe to the "no monopoly" policy advanced
by Conservatives. Monopoly power is not always enlightened; it may
destroy business itself, as large firms act consciously or unconsciously

to protect and expand their influence. Unrestrained business power may in fact subvert government to selfish ends and make the basic principles of property rights and free enterprise subject to special-interest groups. Thus, the creation of a monopoly policy is essential to protect the balance of pluralistic interests in an open society. An equitable balance of labor, consumer, and capital interests must be the philosophical cornerstone of any intelligent policy toward business.

Through fair and calculated government intervention, big business can be made compatible with the social objectives of economic order, reasonable prices and high quality, and technological advancement. Government actions, depending on the situation, must go beyond mere antitrust enforcement. They may take the form of selective tax and subsidy manipulation; more extensive direct controls over pricing, hiring, and capital policies; and direct regulation of such developments as multinational business activity. Monopoly policy, however, must not be separated from general public-policy objectives directed at inflation control, maintaining full employment, and encouraging economic growth. Therefore, social control over specific business actions must be integrated with general macroeconomic policy objectives. Some people will argue that this external imposition of social objectives on the private sector is pure socialism, but they miss the point.

SOCIAL CONTROL IS NOT SOCIALISM

Pragmatic social control of big business is not the same as social ownership. First of all, corporate ownership today is widely dispersed and far removed from the day-to-day management decisions of American business. Excessive concern over *who* owns the productive property only clouds the important business and public issues at stake. *How* the privately owned property is performing is the really important question. Second, even though privately owned, most large businesses are already "social institutions" with "social responsibilities." To put the point simply, GM—with its sales of almost $60 billion and its 700,000 employees—does not have the right to fail any more than it has the right to conspire against the public. To demand social responsibility is perfectly consistent with the real-world structure of business and the economy, and it does not challenge private ownership in any serious way.

Businesses, moreover, are more responsive in the area of social responsibility than is generally understood. Social concern on their part is not purely altruism but good business. Flagrant monopolistic behavior invites government scrutiny and public outrage. The old era of "the public be damned" is past. Few firms, whatever their size and market power, want long and costly antitrust litigation. Even consumer boycotts and public pressure for legislative intervention are sizable threats and induce thoughtful constraint. Moreover, there is significant pressure within the business community to police itself. Abuse of economic power disrupts markets and creates economic instability; this situation, while perhaps favorable to one or a few firms, interferes with general business activity. Social responsibility, finally, is not an ethical question but a matter of profit and loss.

These points should not be misunderstood. The Liberal fully understands that big business indeed may be a threat, in its pricing, labor, international, and other policies. The point is that big business does not have to be a threat to the economic system. It can be brought under social control.

Public policy toward big business, then, remains a matter of directing private enterprise toward social objectives that include reasonable prices, efficiency, high employment, and adequate profit return, while also taking into consideration such broad concerns as ecology, resource conservation, and the overall performance of the economy. The creation of such a policy must be the responsibility of an enlightened federal government. Government must act as an unbiased umpire, attempting always to balance the diverse economic and social interests of the nation. Such intervention need not abridge basic property rights (which is what Radicals want). But it would set social priorities above the pursuit of selfish individualistic goals (so feverishly defended by Conservatives).

The Radical Argument

To some "monopoly power" may seem to be a non-issue. Who, after all, will defend a monopolistic organization of markets? Yet, while both Conservatives and Liberals oppose monopoly power, neither group understands monopoly's place in capitalist development. Neither Conservatives nor Liberals appreciate the present-day scale and political and economic impact of monopoly organization in the

United States, nor do they understand that this phenomenon has not been accidental. Thus the Radical position can be distinguished easily by its interpretation of monopoly as being the centerpiece of modern capitalism and the logical progression of capitalist development. Monopoly power is not merely *a* problem; it is, in the broadest sense, *the problem* of our time. Accordingly, this issue looms much larger for Radicals than for Conservatives or Liberals.

THE ORIGINS AND SCALE OF MONOPOLY DEVELOPMENT

In the early formative stages of capitalist development, competition among many enterprises of relatively similar size and power is the dominant economic characteristic. This is only a temporary and transitional stage, however, not at all the perfect, unchanging economic state of affairs idealized by Conservatives and even some Liberals. The reason that this stage comes to an end is not difficult to explain. Competition ever expands the productive base and cheapens the price of commodities. With falling prices come falling profits. Many competitive capitalists, faced with the frequent periods of general economic crisis that grip a capitalist economy, cannot survive. At first, "gentlemen's agreements" to maintain prices, divide profits, or allocate sales territories may be tried, but these tactics break down as the larger enterprises violate the agreement and drive out the smaller producers. The small are eliminated either through bankruptcy or through merger, but the effect is the same: concentration of production among fewer and fewer producers and centralization of wealth into fewer and fewer hands.

In the process of concentration and centralization, merger remains the favored technique. In the United States, merger activity has occurred in four great waves (see Figure 4.1): 1897–1900, 1924–1930, 1945–1947, and the current stage which dates from about 1960. During the first three periods, mergers were usually horizontal (among producers of a similar product) or vertical (among buyers and sellers in different stages of the production process). The putting together of most American industrial giants took place during these periods of horizontal and vertical mergers. Meanwhile, once size was established, it tended to generate greater size as the dominant firms were able to control prices, technological introduction, and, most significantly, profits to their own growth advantage.

Nowhere is the rate of concentration more evident than in automobiles. The number of independently owned automobile producers fell from 181 in 1900 to forty-four in 1927 to just four by the 1960s. Today, GM alone accounts for about 60 percent of American-made auto and truck sales. Meanwhile, evidence of industry concentration and one-firm dominance is easily evident in even a cursory survey of modern American business: steel (and United States Steel), aluminum (and Alcoa), mainframe computers (and IBM), and so on. In such diverse industries as aircraft, machine tools and instruments, dairy products, baking, industrial chemicals, petroleum refining, rubber, cigarettes, soaps, photographic equipment, and office equipment, the top four firms account for more than half of all output, employment, and profits.

Since the 1960s, practically all mergers have taken a conglomerate form (combining enterprises in wholly unrelated lines of production). While Conservative and Liberal apologists are quick to point out that, with the decline of horizontal and vertical mergers, industrial concentration in particular industries has slowed down, they scarcely recognize the enormous centralization potential of conglomerate mergers. Practically every giant enterprise has diversified into unrelated markets. This, of course, means that a giant such as GM, which is involved in autos, aircraft engines, household consumer products, banking, and much more, can bring its awesome power to bear in more than one market.

The facts of increasing concentration and centralization are stubbornly obvious. As Figure 4.2 indicates, there is no end in sight to the cannibalistic behavior of modern big business. Between 1975 and 1981, giant mergers increased tenfold. Thus, by 1981, the largest 500 manufacturing firms controlled over 70 percent of industrial sales and more than 75 percent of manufacturing employment and profits. Their sales volume was over $1.8 trillion. Looking at corporate concentration and centralization another way, less than 1 percent of all corporations now owned more than 60 percent of all corporate assets.

THE EFFECTS OF MONOPOLY

As every veteran of introductory economics knows, traditional theory holds monopoly power to be disruptive to the economy and society. While conventional economists commonly hold to such theoretical views of monopoly power, few are able to recognize the real

FIGURE 4.2   SEVEN-YEAR GROWTH OF GIANT MERGERS, 1975–1981

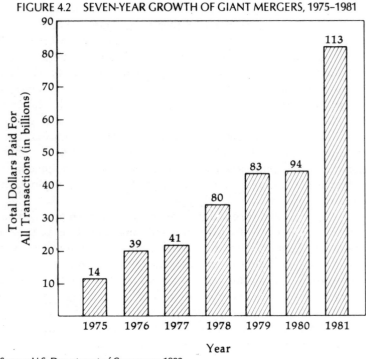

Source: U.S. Department of Commerce, 1982.

thing when they see it. Somehow the present concentration and centralization of economic power is not associated with the monopoly model. Consequently, the real effects of monopoly power on American workers and consumers is overlooked. These adverse effects appear in a variety of forms, from higher prices to fewer jobs and greater political and personal manipulation.

The ability of a firm to earn profits clearly depends upon its size. Billion dollar enterprises earn profit rates about three times larger than million-dollar firms. While it may be argued with some truth that larger size allows for some economies of scale in production and therefore larger profit margins, the phenomenal profit rates of the giants are mostly the result of their monopolistic pricing ability rather than greater efficiency. In fact, in some industries (cars, for example), the habit of setting monopolistic prices first and tending to efficiency questions last is well known and easily demonstrated.

Automobile producers long ago exceeded the economies-of-scale benefits of bigness. Indeed, American business leaders have tacitly admitted the fact. George Romney, then president of American Motors, told a Senate subcommittee in 1958 that in auto production cost economies are a "negligible thing" after 400,000 units per year. At that time, as well as now, all U.S. producers except AMC exceeded that figure. The inefficiency of the giant auto producers became evident in the 1970s and 1980s as foreign competitors grabbed more than a quarter of the American market. As the industry slumped through the recession of 1981–1982 and struggled to keep itself afloat among a flood of foreign imports, workers were furloughed by the tens of thousands.

While the auto industry's difficulties reflect the natural tendencies toward inefficiency in an established monopolistic enterprise, the recent merger movement has produced a special kind of inefficiency. With corporate capital being absorbed in grand merger schemes, little has been made available to expand output and improve production techniques. Again, the worker pays as American products lose ground to foreign competition. (More on this in Issue 7.)

While workers are squeezed from some jobs due to giant firms' productive inefficiency, others are forced into unemployment as concentration and centralization produces a variety of "labor-saving" schemes. In some cases, growth and merger lead directly to more capital-intensive output techniques. (Of course, "capital intensive" is not necessarily to be confused with greater efficiency.) In other cases, the giant simply may close what it considers duplicating operations or relocate them overseas or elsewhere in the United States where wages are lower.

In the old industrial heartland of the Northeast and the Midwest, joblessness resulting from the latter types of monopolistic behavior is well known. The scenario goes like this: First, a small or medium-sized manufacturing operation is picked up by a growing multinational conglomerate. Second, after acquiring the local firm's good name, its market, its patents, and anything else of value, the conglomerate announces that current operations will be "relocated." Third, the plant "runs away" to a new location—often overseas but frequently to safe non-union American sites. While it is possible that some jobs are created elsewhere, the runaway plant leaves massive joblessness and devastated communities in its wake.

Whether jobs have been lost to new production methods, to closing redundant facilities, or to production inefficiencies, the relative stagnation of employment in the big business sector is easily shown. Between 1964 and 1980, the nation's 500 largest industrial firms increased the real value of their capital assets by more than 100 percent; yet, this growth increased their payrolls (and much of this took place overseas) by only 5 million workers, or 30 percent. Looking at the trends another way, the 500 largest industrials increased their share of the nation's output by almost 50 percent but their share of the nation's employment remained constant at about 14 percent. The trend is obvious: As fewer and fewer firms control more and more of American output, they employ relatively fewer workers. More workers are pushed downward into the lower-paying and less-secure bottom rungs of American business and many slip into permanent unemployment.

Meanwhile, the giant enterprises exercise their power beyond the marketplace. Education, from the public school to the university, is organized to fill the labor and consumer needs of big business at a variety of levels. Through such "charitable" foundations as Ford, Rockefeller, Carnegie, and Exxon, acceptable educational and cultural values are subsidized. Such actions, far from being examples of the "social responsibility of big business" so applauded by some Liberals are but self-serving attempts to gain respectability for monopoly power. This fact is blatantly apparent at Exxon, for instance, whose educational foundation is organized as a sub-bureau of the public relations department.

As ITT's attempt in the early 1970s to grab the American Broadcasting Company showed, giant corporations also seek to control the media. Even when such control is not direct, it may be exercised indirectly because of the financial dependence of radio, television, newspapers, and magazines on advertising revenues from big business. When such societal controls by monopolistic enterprise are added to the exploitative economic domination of monopoly power, it is evident that almost every aspect of our lives—on the job or at leisure—is molded by the needs of giant corporations.

Nor is the influence of monopoly capitalism limited to the national boundaries of capitalist nations. In the case of the United States, its growth and expansion as an imperialist power almost exactly paralleled the centralization and concentration of capital. The same ceaseless drive to accumulate surplus and profits that led to monopoly development soon forced American entrepreneurs beyond their borders in search of markets, cheap labor, or raw materials. The burden of monopoly is felt around the world.

THE FAILURE OF GOVERNMENT

Given this grim picture of the giants' domination, can we construct a policy to alleviate the problem? If by a policy we mean some enlarged form of government antitrust enforcement, the answer is no. The tail does not wag the dog. Corporate domination of government is perhaps the most obvious example of naked monopoly power. It is hoped that this fact is becoming more widely appreciated by the mass of citizens. As Marx said, "The state is the form in which individuals of a ruling class assert their common interests." The power of business interests to dominate government dates back to the writing of the Constitution; however, it has been most obvious since the rise of the trusts and modern corporations. Business has been able to create regulatory agencies in its own interest (the Interstate Commerce Commission, for instance) and to have the antitrust laws used as antilabor devices. Even after antitrust law finally was directed against business, it was used to halt concentrations of business power in only the most flagrant cases of malignant monopoly. The recent Justice Department decision that IBM's 65-percent share of the mainframe computer business did not violate antitrust law should serve to prove that big business has little to fear from so-called "trust busting."

We already have discussed how automakers have used and manipulated consumer protection laws, how agribusiness has created governmental farm policy, how energy companies have enlisted government to establish higher energy prices. Perhaps no recent event better illustrates the degree of integration between government and big business than the government's bail-out of Chrysler Corporation. With more than $2 billion in tax moneys "loaned" to this poorly managed giant, the "risks" of capital have now been shouldered by ordinary citizen-taxpayers. As we shall continue to see, the manipulation of government by monopolistic business enterprise is natural to our economic organization. Neutrality is simply not possible for a government that depends on business support to elect its officials and is formally committed to the production-for-profit system. While Liberals may argue that social control and accountability are their goal, this is nonsense if the maintenance of capitalism as a system is a prior and overriding objective.

The solution to the monopoly problem does not lie within the framework of conventional economic analysis and policy. The only humane solution is social ownership and operation of the means of production. This means participation by individual workers and control by workers as a whole over such basic economic questions as what goods shall be produced, how, and for whom. In terms of immediate Radical strategy, this means support for all efforts leading to greater worker control over production, profits, and wages. Worker planning, not corporate planning, is the final objective; however, such planning must be coordinated with the needs of the entire society. For those who sneer at such proposals as "pie in the sky," it should be pointed out that models of labor-managed systems are in place and thriving in Sweden, Yugoslavia, and other countries.

ISSUE 5

The Economics of Regulation and Deregulation
Which Policy for American Railroads?

The committee has found among the leading representatives of the railroad interests an increasing readiness to accept the aid of Congress in working out the solution of the railroad problem which has obstinately baffled all their efforts, and not a few of the ablest railroad men of the country seem disposed to look to the intervention of Congress as promising to afford the best means of ultimately securing a more equitable and satisfactory adjustment of the relations of the transportation interests to the community than they themselves have been able to bring about.

U.S. Senate Select Committee on Interstate Commerce, 1886

The ICC is now primarily a forum at which private transportation interests settle their disputes. . . . As a passive forum the ICC has failed to provide for any useful . . . representation of the public interest.

Ralph Nader Study Group, 1970

Railroads were totally regulated for almost a century. Obviously it will take time for railroads to learn all of the things that can be done in a freer climate. It will also take shippers time to learn this as well. But already it is apparent that both can use deregulation to their respective advantages.

Association of American Railroads, 1982

THE PROBLEM

Even before the Sherman Anti-Trust Act established the legal rules and the machinery for controlling monopoly abuses, Congress recognized that some industries should be "protected" from competition. In 1887, the Interstate Commerce Commission (ICC) was established to oversee the nation's struggling railroad industry. Over the next century, more than a dozen independent regulatory agencies and commissions were created to control business activities in everything from banking to using the airwaves to nuclear power. Meanwhile, hundreds of state agencies also were created to regulate certain industries within states' borders.

The long-held logic of insulating certain industries from the market applied in two general cases: "natural monopoly" and "partial competition." In the case of a natural monopoly, such as a local telephone company or a natural-gas company, the regulated firm would be required to provide specified service at specified rates. At the same time the firm would be protected by the regulatory agency from competitors entering the market. Costly competition would be avoided and the public interest would be protected at the same time.

Our consideration of public regulation, however, will focus on the second case: partial competition. A partially competitive firm, such as a railroad, has both monopoly characteristics (one among several railroads operating between two or more cities) and competitive characteristics (one among several railroads and other transporters operating between two or more cities). In such a case, public regulation supposedly should protect vulnerable consumers from the firm's monopoly power and protect the firm from the anarchy of cutthroat competition, which might break out periodically and weaken the firm's ability to maintain operations. Again, desired levels of service and fair rates would be prescribed by a regulatory agency committed to protecting both the public interest and the regulated industry.

In theory the traditional approach to public regulation of certain industries seems reasonable enough. No one appears to be a loser. Recently, however, a considerable grassroots pressure has developed that urges an end to much of the regulatory activities that were once taken for granted. Some extremists would end all regulation, even in the areas of natural monopolies; however, most proponents of deregulation stop well short of that position, applying deregulation only to partially competitive firms.

Deregulation has proceeded fairly swiftly in the transportation industries. Airlines were deregulated in 1978. Since 1978, there has been gradual deregulation in railroads, and trucking deregulation began in 1980. Evidence is mixed as to whether ending regulatory authority strengthens the economy or not. In the case of the airlines, deregulation, plus rising fuel costs and a recession, have lowered carriers' profits. Similarly, many truckers have shown a wariness of deregulation. However, the railroad industry has embraced the end of ICC authority with special enthusiasm. From the point of view of many railroaders, regulation was instrumental in the railroads' fall from transportation dominance and things had become so bad that virtually any policy change was welcomed.

The deregulation advocates are bound to extend their efforts beyond transportation in the future. Consequently, the transportation case, and especially the case of the railroads, is instructive—both in looking back at the causes and effects of regulation but also in looking ahead to the possible merits or demerits of a broad national policy that would end an experiment that began nearly one hundred years ago with the ICC.

In looking at the nation's oldest regulated industry, some reference points are needed. As Figure 5.1 indicates, railroads simply dominated American transportation before the 1930s. Over the last half-century, however, even though railroad freight tonnage has been growing, railroads have suffered a precipitous decline in their share of the transportation market. Between 1930 and 1980, their proportion of freight movement fell from 80 percent to about 35 percent.

In ruin or not, railroads remain far more important than most Americans realize.* Although their traffic shares have fallen, they move more freight today than during the boom years of gasolineless World War II. Important industries and entire lines of commodities are dependent upon railroads; therefore, the future of the railroad industry and the proper role

---

*As the energy crisis deepens, the importance of the railroads to the national transportation network should grow. Approximately three times as fuel efficient as trucks in moving freight, railroads should enjoy a growing fuel cost advantage. In fact, a combination of rising fuel prices and creeping deregulation produced a sharp upturn in railroad earnings in 1979, practically doubling profits from 1978 levels. Whether or not this signifies a permanent change in rail fortunes remains to be seen. See *Forbes*, January 7, 1980, pp. 161–167.

FIGURE 5.1   SHARES OF INTERCITY FREIGHT TRAFFIC BY CARRIER,
1930–1980

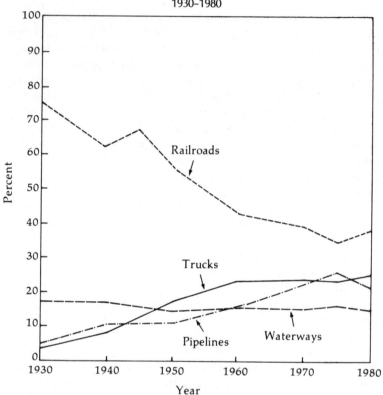

Source: Association of American Railroads, Yearbook of Railroad Facts, 1980.

of government toward that industry are pertinent problems. As we shall see, however, there is wide disagreement among our representative schools of thought as to the significance and direction of past and current rail regulation trends.

SYNOPSIS. The Conservative argument states that regulation is counterproductive, harming society's welfare and weakening the regulated industry. The Liberal argument defends regulation as the only possible alternative to the market chaos that industries like railroads otherwise would face. The Radical argument sees regulatory efforts as merely another prop for monopoly privileges and proposes nationalization of all public transportation.

Anticipating the Arguments

- What are some of the counterproductive results of railroad regulation that Conservatives see, and how would their plan for deregulation end such problems?

- On what grounds do Liberals defend at least limited regulation over complete deregulation?

- Why do Radicals reject regulation and instead call for public ownership and operation of railroads?

The Conservative Argument

The Conservative position on the ICC, railroads, and regulation in general is based on two sturdy and now-familiar principles. First, regulation—or any interference with the market—tends to create resource misallocation, inefficiency, and, ultimately, greater costs to the community. Second, left alone, the market is capable of more rational decisions about the success or survival of a firm or industry than is the voting public or its representatives and bureaucrats.

THE FAILURE OF REGULATION

The creation of federal and state regulatory agencies under the guise of "improving" the performance of the market has had precisely the opposite effect. By making pricing and resource allocation matters of committee decision, all the natural checks on inefficiency are eliminated. The "right" price and the proper allocation of goods, labor, and capital are now merely matters of "administration." But administration, regardless of how noble its motives or how efficient its marshaling of evidence, is at best a hit-and-miss process.

Probably the best known example of regulatory failure has been the ICC. As our oldest regulatory agency, it has the longest list of failures and is a good example of all the debilitating effects that age brings to commission activity. The original intent of the ICC was to bring order to the chaotic and excessively competitive rate-making practices of the railroads. Its goal was to protect the public from railroad price collusion and to protect the railroads from one another. By the mid 1930s, ICC power extended to all surface commercial transportation in the country. Specific ICC controls covered rate setting, merger, financial issues, abandonment, and service discontinuance, as well as carrier layoffs of labor. There was virtually nothing that a rail carrier or any other carrier regulated by the Interstate Commerce Commission could do without first obtaining commission approval.

How well has the ICC performed its regulatory task? The proof of the pudding is in the eating. Today most of the American railroad industry is in serious trouble. Most of the lines in the Northeast are in bankruptcy or have become part of the federal rescue effort known as Conrail Corporation. Passengers are left to the tender mercies of the government's Amtrak, which operates what is left of a once-splendid intercity passenger network. Across the nation, railroad earnings on both capital and sales remain, as they have been through most of this century, extremely low. Capital is not attracted, although it is badly needed.

Though still the primary movers of commodities, railroads have lost ground steadily to trucks, air freight, and water transport alternatives. Under an ICC mandate to operate in the "public interest," railroads have been required to offer services and charge rates that continue to erode their capital position and their ability to compete with other forms of transportation. The physical deterioration of tracks and equipment is hard to appreciate because it is so staggering. In much of the Northeast, on tracks where fast freights cruised at 50 to 60 miles an hour a half-century ago, average speeds have been reduced to 20 to 25 miles an hour, and even these speeds may be dangerous.

The ICC is not the sole cause of railroad deterioration, of course. The government's decision to subsidize truck, air, and water transportation by building and maintaining their "roadbeds" (highways, airports, and canals) gave these transport alternatives an unfair advantage over the heavily taxed railroads. Certainly the railroads would profit from more equitable subsidies and taxes. But the ICC has made a bad problem worse.

In misguided efforts to "maintain competition among different modes," the ICC long followed the strategy of "umbrella rate making," a practice of setting a rate high enough to allow less efficient modes of transport to earn a profit on specific service. This provided a special handicap to railroads which lost traffic to other modes simply because they were not allowed to set lower rates (prices) and utilize their greater efficiency in certain goods movement. In protecting trucks and water carriers, the railroads saw the ICC direct business away from them. Meanwhile, shippers and consumers absorbed higher than needed transport charges in their purchases.

Similar anticompetitive outcomes have resulted from the ICC's past opposition to rail mergers. This led to costly "balkanization." The 400 line haul railroads were unable to combine to increase freight exchange and coordination and to strengthen their financial structures. By denying the industry access to these economies of scale, service remained expensive and inefficient. At the same time the ICC also prohibited intermodal mergers. Railroads were not allowed to consolidate with trucks and other carriers to improve their overall efficiency.

Meanwhile, in search of the will-o'-the-wisp "public interest," the ICC also acted to raise transport costs and reduce rail efficiency by maintaining redundant routes and little-used spurs. Permission for abandonments of low-density or loss-producing operations were difficult to obtain from the commission, and railroads were compelled to pour millions of dollars into expensive routes that generated only a few dollars in traffic.

By prohibiting railroads from setting their rates freely, denying them the right to develop joint rail–truck transportation companies, and demanding that they continue to operate costly and inefficient services and schedules, the ICC rendered the railroads' competitive situation virtually hopeless. ICC decisions on rates, abandonments, and mergers were presented as proof of the agency's commitment to the public interest. In point of fact, its actions harmed rather than protected the nation's welfare.

THE MARKET ALTERNATIVE

What might have happened if railroads, buses, airplanes, and trucks had never been regulated? Certainly the overbuilt American railroad network of the 1900s would have contracted. There never was a good economic reason for a quadruple-tracked main line between New York and Chicago, and many other roads were laid without any economic justification at all. On the other hand, buses, trucks, and private autos would not have offered such a competitive threat to railroads if they had not been subsidized at the same time that railroads were being heavily taxed. Before the collapse of the Penn-Central in the early 1970s, the president of the railroad ruefully reported to Congress that, parallel to and within sight of the main line through New York's Hudson Valley, there were two state highways, one interstate highway, and a state canal system; overhead was a federally subsidized air corridor. Profit making was indeed tough for a private railroad under such circumstances.

We might speculate that, left to the dictates of a free market, a national transportation mix might have emerged that would have allowed each transport mode to develop its inherent strengths. Instead of the artificial competition that pitted trucks and railroads against each other but provided no way of determining their relative efficiency, each form of transportation could have exploited its own advantages, dropping out of markets where it had none. The present transportation crisis never would have developed if the market had been allowed to determine pricing and operational advantage.

A NEW DIRECTION: DEREGULATION OF TRANSPORTATION

By the late 1970s, the failed record of ICC regulation and the continued economic problems of the railroads prompted a new direction in government railroad policy: deregulation of the railroad industry. This development, however, was only part of a broader policy redirection: the gradual deregulation of all commercial transportation, including airlines and truckers as well as railroads.

After passage of the Airline Deregulation Acts of 1977 and 1978, the Civil Aeronautics Board (CAB) was the first of the transportation regulatory agencies to move in the new direction. Under the new laws, air carriers were granted greater rate-making freedom and greater freedom to enter or exit from airline markets. In the past, the CAB had maintained the same regulatory inefficiency in the air as its ICC counterpart had done on land. Now the CAB allowed the industry to fly on a "first-come, first-served" basis to most American cities. The action ended the old and inefficient practice of granting virtual monopoly power to certain carriers over some routes. As a result, dozens of old companies altered their routes (both expanding and contracting service on specific routes). At the same time, a score or more of brand-new long-distance carriers suddenly appeared. Meanwhile, the market, rather than the CAB, was allowed to determine most airline rates. The new approach brought most long-distance air fares down. At the same time, loss-producing routes were abandoned to new specialized commuter lines or fares were adjusted upward by the larger carriers to reflect real operating costs. The newfound market freedom allowed the airlines to price and operate according to actual supply-and-demand conditions and permitted the passenger to enjoy the price benefits of competition.

Two years after the deregulation of the airlines, the Motor Carrier Act of 1980 brought gradual deregulation to the trucking industry (regulated by the ICC since 1930). Again the approach was the same: to allow greater freedom in rate making by individual truckers and the easing of entry restrictions into long-haul, interstate trucking. The benefits to the public came quickly. More than 5200 new trucking firms entered the industry in the first 18 months of deregulation; 20,000 new route applications were filed with the ICC; and average freight bills went down 10 to 20 percent.

The centerpiece to transportation deregulation, however, was the railroad industry. Could deregulation in fact return the industry to a place of economic strength and efficiency? While not all the votes are in, the early returns show a resounding victory for deregulation.

The first efforts at railroad deregulation have been provided through two important acts, the Railroad Revitalization and Regulation Reform Act of 1976 (the 4-R Act) and the Staggers Rail Act of 1980. With its creation of Conrail (to operate the six bankrupt railroads of the Northeast) and its provisions for enlarged federal financing for railroads, the 4-R Act still evaded a pure market solution to rail problems. Nevertheless, it did reduce the regulatory powers of the ICC. The act committed the regulatory agency to a philosophy of price flexibility in rate setting, allowing roads greater freedom in setting their own rates rather than laboring under an imposed ICC rate. Meanwhile, the act encouraged railroad mergers and eased restrictions on abandoning low-revenue and loss-producing operations. While the rail network and the number of operating railroads have declined under 4-R, competition actually has increased as merged railroads have grown stronger and are challenging other subsidized modes of transportation more effectively.

The 1980 Staggers Act broadened the 4-R efforts. In particular, railroads were freed to make most rate changes without prior ICC approval and also were given permission to contract directly with shippers at less-than-market rates for long-term, bulk shipments. Previously, the prior approval for rate changes had cost the railroads up to $1 billion a year as the ICC delayed adjusting rates for inflation. In the past, special shipper–railroad contracts had been held to be an illegal form of rebating.

From the Conservative point of view, such deregulation in the railroad industry (and transportation in general) is only a beginning. The ICC still retains final authority over many areas of rate making and maintenance of service (as it does also over trucking and as the CAB does over airlines). As a result, we cannot say that the rail industry finally has been deregulated. However, the recent trend is important. More deregulation should follow as both the society and the railroads gain from the reduction of regulatory interference. Who says it is impossible to roll back all that federal bureaucracy and get back to market basics?

The Liberal Argument

Regulatory agencies are the logical outcome of the need to improve market conditions in certain industries. Direct regulation is not essential to all market conditions, but in certain cases—mainly where natural monopolies tend to develop or should be encouraged—regulation by government agencies can maximize the benefits of both the consumer and the affected industry. Antitrust action, as we have noted earlier, is employed in cases of conspiracy to attain a socially undesirable monopoly advantage in the market, but direct regulation is a ratification of monopoly power. In exchange for this recognized monopoly position, a firm submits itself to close political and economic supervision.

THE "RULES" OF REGULATION

Under regulation, business firms are guaranteed certain rights. For example, their property rights are legally protected and confiscation is not a serious possibility. They are entitled to receive reasonable prices and a fair rate of return on their capital. In the specific geographical area in which it operates, a regulated firm is given partial or total protection from competition. A firm can challenge in the courts any regulating decision made by the relevant commission.

Regulated firms also have certain obligations. Their prices and profits must not be excessive. Prices should be established so as to offer the greatest possible service without compelling a company to forfeit its capital through continuous losses. Moreover, the regulated firm must meet all demand at the prices established. Any change in the quantity or quality of service (in the case of the railroads, this means especially the abandonment of service) must be approved in advance by the regulatory agency. The final decision in such cases as railroad petitions for abandonment of track or service must balance two conflicting objectives: the firm's operational benefits and the public interest. Finally, all regulated industries must be committed to high levels of performance with the highest possible standards of safety to the public. The key to regulation philosophy which has developed through nine decades of experience and sixteen independent agencies is this: a balance of public and private (corporate) interests.

The American experience with regulatory agencies is long enough, especially in the case of railroads and the ICC, so that we can judge how well they work. Admittedly, the evidence is mixed. Regulation has not always provided a fair balance between carriers and the public. But the record is not altogether bad. An accurate judgment of the worth of regulation might be reached best by asking what would have happened in its absence. In terms of railroads and the ICC, how might commercial transportation have developed without regulation? Does the Conservative argument for a purely "market solution" have much basis in fact?

RAILROADS AND THE ICC

Railroads were America's first big business. By the late 1880s, more than 150,000 miles of main-line trackage had been built. Railroads reported their current book value of investment at about $8 billion. (To understand the significance of this investment, we should note that the GNP in 1890 has been estimated at about $13 billion.) The 750,000 railroad workers represented more than 5 percent of the nation's nonfarm employment. Millions more were employed indirectly by the railroads in steel, machine tool, rolling stock, and related industries. Added to this, the commercial interaction facilitated by railroads had stimulated investment and created jobs all across the nation, jobs that had not existed before the railroads came to town.

For all this apparent vitality, railroads were in trouble. Most had been built in advance of traffic demand. Many were purely speculative roads, laid down by promoters with an eye to quick profits from construction and from securities sales. Railroads, especially in the Northeast and Midwest, paralleled and duplicated routes. In almost every case, they were overcapitalized. Debt payments and dividend expectations simply outstripped the corporations' real earning power. To summarize, the industry was suffering from excess capacity and excessive capitalization. Big as it was, the economic foundation of the railroads was laid on shifting sands.

Periodically, bloody rate wars would break out among the giants as each tried to gain a larger share of the restricted transportation market. As a result, there were frequent bankruptcies and breakdowns in service. Because of their critical central place in the economy, as railroads went, so went the nation. Every major financial panic and recession after the Civil War—in 1873, 1884, and 1893—started with railroad bankruptcies. Attempts at private rate-fixing and cartels, even before their unconstitutionality was established by the Sherman Anti-Trust Act, almost always failed. Even so, these expedients harmed farmers and other shippers. This, then, was the situation when the ICC was created in 1887. The free-market operation of the rail industry no longer could be tolerated. This view was held widely by bankers, farmers, shippers, and railroad management.

Space does not permit a detailed description of the gradual elaboration of ICC authority. It is sufficient to say that the initial limited powers of the commission over rate setting were enlarged to cover virtually all operations of railroads operating in interstate commerce. Eventually all commercial surface transport enterprises came under ICC jurisdiction. The accretions of power in every case were responses to the failure of competitive market operations in the transport industry.

With regard to the railroads, the ICC has basically been preoccupied with the industry's chronic excess capacity problems, since virtually all rail problems are traceable to this difficulty. During the 1920s, even before trucks offered serious competition, the ICC tried to encourage the merger of American railroads into a limited number of systems (four or five systems for the entire Northeast, for instance). The railroads successfully fought this plan, and consolidation came only in the wake of financial collapse in the 1950s and 1960s. Meanwhile, the ICC permitted a 20-percent reduction in main-line trackage from the peak of 254,000 miles in 1916. It allowed railroads to end expensive partial-carload shipments and permitted the virtual elimination of passenger service. As truck competition grew, the commission attempted to price the services of this rival so as to hold up railroad revenues and assure adequate returns. While not all ICC actions were rapid or supportive enough to suit rail management, it cannot be said that the ICC was indifferent to railroad needs. Moreover, in all its actions the commission considered the public interest—a factor in which the railroads had no natural concern.

In many cases ICC actions were inadequate. In the high-density traffic of the Northeast, no rating policy or abandonment policy could save the Penn-Central. Burdened by a merciless debt structure, challenged on all sides by state-subsidized truck competition, and plagued by plain bad management, the road collapsed in 1970.

Despite the current problems of the railroad industry, it is not fair to single out the ICC as a major cause of railroad crisis. Nor is it correct to conclude by implication that government regulatory commissions are failures. The ICC was not responsible for the rail industry's excess capacity or excessive capitalization. Neither was it responsible for the growth of truck competition or the proliferation of the private passenger car.

"DEREGULATION" RECONSIDERED

From the Liberal point of view, then, past railroad regulation is defensible. If there are troubles with regulation, it is because we have moved too slowly to develop a national transportation plan. The ICC was charged only with executing, not making, national transportation policy. The ICC has balanced as best it could the public interest in cheap and available transportation with the private goal of obtaining profits. Critics of the regulatory system who proclaim the market to be a better determinant of price and quality might well be right in saying that an unregulated transport system would earn more profits—at least for a few firms. What then would happen to the public interest? Who would protect the public against unrestrained monopoly power?

The provision of transportation services is simply too important to be left to the market. What is needed is a national transportation plan. While Conservatives may see the recent 4-R Act (Railroad Revitalization and Regulatory Reform Act of 1976) as a new direction, they fail to grasp its real significance—an attempt to develop a more rationally planned national transportation network. Far from abandoning railroads to the unregulated whims of the market, the 4-R Act was a large step in developing a national transportation plan. The chaos in the Northeast, largely the result of past market failures, was replaced by Conrail, a government-organized merger of the six bankrupt roads. However, in this reorganization the principle of private ownership was retained, for Contrail eventually was to become, after a necessary period of government subsidy and reorganization, a private for-profit rail operation. Certainly the market could not have facilitated such a maintenance of private ownership in the rail industry.

In addition, the 4-R Act provided funds for the capital improvement of railroads, expanded the power of the Interstate Commerce Commission over intrastate rates, ended discriminatory taxation by separate states on rail property, and provided for the reorganization and streamlining of ICC decision making. Moreover, the act recognized the importance of developing new approaches to intermodal competition between railroads and other transportation modes. 4-R was a step forward toward improved regulation, not the end of regulation.

Regrettably, the most recent transportation legislation reflects an abandonment of these principles. The Staggers Act, the Airline Deregulation Act, and the recent Motor Carrier Act went too far in reducing regulatory power, or in instituting "deregulation." This attempt to march into the past seems to promise greater transportation problems for Americans than free-market advocates realize.

In the case of airlines and trucking, the greater rate-making and entry and exit freedoms have caused the reappearance of a cutthroat competition reiminiscent of the "bad old" railroad era. Airlines have seen prices on competitive routes fall below costs, and riders on high-priced monopoly routes stop flying. As a result, 1981 and 1982 produced the greatest two-year losses in the airlines' history. Meanwhile, the "deregulated" trucking industry watched profits fall by 50 percent between 1978 and 1982. Emerging financial problems for deregulated airlines and truckers may produce the same scenario that railroads underwent a century ago: first, a series of bankruptcies with their attendant loss of services; followed by a round of mergers; and, finally, monopolistic rate-setting policies. If we recall the railroad scenario we might just remember why regulatory commissions were established in the first place.

The rush to deregulate has not yet destroyed the regulatory base in transportation. The ICC is still alive and well, with considerable regulatory powers. If the ICC's and other agencies' regulatory powers are improved and adapted to meet the requirements of a broad-based national transportation policy, regulation and transportation can enter a new era built upon past successes rather than one in which they are damned to repeat past errors.

The Radical Argument

Public regulatory commissions were organized in modern monopoly capitalism to ratify the existence of monopoly. Not only that, but such commissions—regardless of the intention of reformers who championed their development—worked primarily on behalf of the industries they regulated. The creation of the ICC, its development in the Progressive Era (1900–1920), and events of the past fifty years do not support the Liberal claim that "public interest" is a major element in regulatory action. Neither do they support the Conservative charge that regulation has been "anti-business."

Ironically, the recent trend toward "deregulation" is only a continuation of the trend toward greater monopoly power. Far from being a return to some halcyon era of competition, deregulation offers certain industries, the railroads for instance, the opportunity to unleash the concentrated economic power that government regulation created. Viewed this way, the free-market/regulation/deregulation oscillations are not a cycle, as conventional economists suggest, but rather the straight-line development of ever greater capital concentration in the United States.

THE ICC AS A CREATURE OF INDUSTRY

Progressive Era legislation and regulatory enactments, rather than being simple-minded efforts to "compromise" the differences of parties on either side of a particular market (as the then-current political rhetoric maintained), were really efforts to bring order to highly disrupted and overly competitive markets. But "order" was achieved on terms that supported the principle of private property and corporate profit-seeking, terms that replaced competition with official recognition of limited monopolistic power and the principle of cartelization.

The ICC from its very beginning was an attempt to create an official cartel in rail transportation. This policy was steadily enlarged and elaborated upon by the industry. Eventually, it also was applied to other modes of public transportation (buses, trucks, water carriers, and pipelines under the ICC and air carriers under the Civil Aeronautics Board). The development of the ICC was not a haphazard abandonment of high principles, but rather the unfolding of a planned and rational policy. (It was rational at least in the sense that it consistently pursued clear ends, even though they might ultimately result in economic and social loss to the nation.)

Although many economic interests favored the creation of a federal railroad regulatory agency in the late 1880s, one of the most influential groups consisted of railroad leaders themselves. The closing decades of the nineteenth century had witnessed costly rate wars and other competitive difficulties, resulting largely from the enormous excess capacity built into the industry. These conflicts could not be dealt with through private efforts at cartelization, partly because these efforts usually collapsed of their own enforcement weaknesses and partly because other economic groups challenged such blatant attempts to build monopoly power. The railroads therefore turned to the federal government and official sanction of cartel creation. Progress toward this end began with passage of the Commerce Act of 1887; over the next twenty years, in the ICC and in Congress, railroads obtained important recognition as a cartel. Indeed, the Elkins Act (1903), which ended the hated competitive practice of paying rebates to certain shippers, was written in the legal offices of the Pennsylvania Railroad. The Hepburn Act (1906), which enlarged the ICC's power, supposedly at the expense of the rail monopolies, had considerable management endorsement.

"Community of interest" (informal domination of all rail operations in a region by a few large roads) and other plans formulated to integrate rail properties for the purpose of obtaining greater monopoly power were frustrated for a time, but railroads emerged from World War I, after their ignominious operational collapse and more than two years of government control, with the Esch-Cummins Act of 1920. This law, as interpreted by the ICC and the courts, firmly established the principle of railroad cartelization. The old competitive situation within the industry existed no longer, and the rail network was reduced to a limited number of essentially noncompetitive systems. Most state regulatory powers over finance and operations were abolished. The old ambition of industry pooling and rate bureaus was given nourishment during the Depression. During the disastrous 1930s, the government, at Franklin Roosevelt's insistence, extended the courtesy of officially recognizing as the industry-wide policy-making body the Association of American Railroads, a powerful lobbyist and a tool for encouraging collusion within the industry. At the behest of rail leaders, the government moved in 1935 to control competition from the hated trucks and buses by placing them under ICC regulatory control. Finally, with the passage of the Transportation Act of 1940, the federal government officially declared an end to any pretense of maintaining "costly competition," either between railroads or among competing transport modes.

None of these regulative and legislative successes by the railroads, however, could insulate the industry from competition and from structural and demand dislocations that persistently wreaked havoc with railroad balance sheets through the 1950s and 1960s. The decline was not halted even by the hastily drawn Transportation Act of 1958, which took away the last effective regulatory power of the states over passenger trains, or by the ICC's growing willingness to approve virtually any kind of merger or abandonment. The railroads had succeeded in getting themselves established as a protected cartel. Though they were not totally free to undertake whatever was in their interest, the official commitment to maintaining railroads as a privately owned industry meant that railroad legislation and regulation were loaded in their favor. The industry had to be kept going—on its own terms. For the society, this translated into the reduction of rail service and the steady deterioration of what remained.

INTERPRETING THE RECENT EFFORTS TO "RESCUE" THE RAILROADS

Over the past decade, two apparently contradictory policies have been followed in recent transportation legislation. On the one hand, there was the Rail Revitalization and Regulatory Reform Act of 1976; on the other hand were the various transportation "deregulation" acts. On closer examination, however, it is apparent that these policies had one thing in common: They were exactly what the rail industry wanted. As Conservatives accurately proclaimed, the 4-R Act was written largely on the industry's own terms. In the name of increasing competition, the legislation was intended to stimulate merger, abandonment, and greater freedom by carriers in price setting. Meanwhile the ICC was retooled to give "public-interest" blessing to new private efforts at profit maximization.

In many respects the emergency legislation efforts to deal with the rail crisis in the Northeast corridor reveal the actual content, past and present, of our transportation and regulatory policy. Under the 1976 Regulatory Act, the six bankrupt northeastern railroads were organized into Conrail. Two points are noteworthy in this development. First, Conrail, although federally organized, was to become a private production-for-profit corporation after it had been reconditioned by a massive infusion of government funds and by ruthless reduction in its trackage. Second, Conrail was devised to rescue the funds of the bankrupt railroads' investors. Although the initial government estimate of the scrap value of the bankrupt roads was set at $621 million, the owners claimed their deteriorated rolling stock and rusting rails to be worth at least $7 billion. Under pressure from banks, insurance companies, and other holders of railroad securities, Conrail was initially granted $2.1 billion in federal funds to acquire the nearly worthless financial paper of these roads. As of this writing, individual stockholder and bondholder suits promise to vastly increase this figure. The prospects of monetary gain from Conrail were evident to the investors in the bankrupt lines, many of whom spoke glowingly of government ownership. There was little talk of such actions being "socialistic," but John Kenneth Galbraith has correctly called it "socialism for the rich." At first glance, the recent "deregulation" acts might seem to repudiate the Radical case, to suggest that Radicals somehow want it both ways. In fact, the acts only reflect a new kind of government–railroad agreement. Deregulating transportation in the 1980s can only help the railroads, just as regulation helped in an earlier stage. With rising energy costs and limited government funds to maintain the highway system, deregulation gives railroads a major cost advantage over trucks. Regulation earlier protected railroads from competition between themselves and the highly subsidized truckers. Now, with the railroad industry highly concentrated (and few new railroads likely to be built), intermodal competition will create rail domination of trucking. The less concentrated trucking industry already is feeling the effect as their profits fall and rail profits rise. In the railroad–truck competition, giant transportation firms will be built on the railroad stem as railroads add their own trucking facilities at either end of their rail routes. For awhile there may be an illusion of competition (more truckers, more rate freedom, and so on), but the competition only masks the development of new monopoly power in the transportation industry.

A DIFFERENT ALTERNATIVE

With greater market concentration and reduced regulative controls (the likely scenario for the railroad industry of the future), the necessity for immediate and decisive resolution of "the railroad problem" is obvious. With railroads undergoing a financial and operating renaissance during the current "deregulation" era, the old arguments of nationalizing the railroads to keep them operating has little persuasive effect. *The point is to nationalize all forms of public transportation and to create a transport network that is free of monopoly control and capable of meeting the entire society's needs.* If we can admit that idea into our discussion long enough, perhaps the fancies and myths we harbor about attempts to balance private and public interest may be revealed and understood for what they are.

Under a socially owned and operated transportation system we also could address a host of other problems that spin off from our present production-for-profit transportation network. Such important problems as air and noise pollution, crowded and inaccessible inner cities, wasteful suburban sprawl, and the surrender of more open space to the inexorable advance of concrete and asphalt could be dealt with under a socially planned transportation system.

Social ownership—not mere "social control" of private property—is the lesson to be learned from the experience of the railroads and the Interstate Commerce Commission. Nor need the lesson be limited in application merely to the railroad problem.

Labor Problems
Are the Unions Too Powerful?

We, the members of the National Association of Manufacturers of the United States of America . . . do hereby declare the following principles. . . . (1) that fair dealing is the fundamental and basic principle on which relations between employees and employers should rest. . . . (6) Employers must be unmolested and unhampered in the management of their business, in determining the amount and quality of their product, and in the use of any methods or systems of pay which are just and equitable.
Statement of Principles, N.A.M., 1903

In the profit sharing scheme, we're trying to find a rational means by which free labor and free management, sitting at the bargaining table, can attempt to work out in their relationship practical means by which you can equate the competing equities—in workers, stockholders, and consumers.
Walter Reuther, United Auto Workers, CIO, 1958

TIME TABLE OF THE HOLYOKE MILLS
(to take effect on or after Jan. 3d, 1853)

Morning Bells . . . first bell at 4:40 A.M.
    yard gates open at ringing of bells for ten minutes
Breakfast Bells . . . ring out at 7 A.M.; ring in at 7:30 A.M.
Dinner Bells . . . ring out at 12:30 P.M.; ring in at 1 P.M.
Evening Bells . . . ring out at 6:30 P.M.*
*excepting on Saturdays when the sun sets previous to 6:30.
    At such times ring out at sunset. (in all cases the first
    stroke of the bell is considered as the marking time)
Posted Hours of a Massachusetts Mill, 1853

THE PROBLEM

Although the labor-union movement can be traced back to colonial times, the development of unions as a political and economic force is comparatively new. As recently as seventy years ago, unions were fought in the courts and, failing that, the streets, by employers who were unwilling to relinquish their traditional power over the workforce. The bloody conflicts between union organizers and strikebreakers hired by stubborn business owners remain an unpleasant page in American history. Not until the 1930s did labor unions receive a feeble mandate from government (under the Wagner Act of 1935) to organize and collectively bargain with management. However, as Figure 6.1 shows, the New Deal years were a golden period for American unions, with membership growing by more than 300 percent—from 4 million members in 1934 to over 15 million by 1942.

By the end of World War II, unions were firmly established in all basic American industries—steel, autos, petrochemicals, construction, and transportation. Moreover, the unions' political clout was a formidable force in American politics. Working closely with the Democratic party in the postwar years, the AFL-CIO and a number of other large independents helped to shape government policy toward unions and other social policies affecting labor. Welfare, Social Security, job programs, and minimum-wage legislation all bear the imprint of organized labor.

The rising economic and political influence of organized labor was not welcomed in all quarters. While few opponents of labor really contested a union's rights to organize, many believed that the courts and legislation had gone too far, creating an imbalance in labor–management negotiations that greatly favored labor. These Conservative attacks upon organized labor became louder and more persuasive in the stagnating economy of the 1970s and early 1980s. With profits low and prices rising, many non-union Americans came to agree with the charge that unions were harming the economy. To make matters worse for unions, it became apparent that their strength was not as great as they perhaps had believed. With slightly more than 20 million members in 1982, unions could claim only about 22 percent of all American workers as members. Moreover, their old strength—unionization of the basic industries—had turned into a weakness. These "basic industries" had ceased to grow and as their place in the American economy declined so did union influence

FIGURE 6.1   UNION MEMBERSHIP, 1900–1980

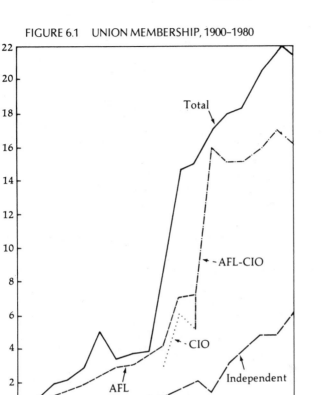

Source: U.S. Bureau of the Census, *Historical Statistics of the United States*, 1976, p. 389, and the U.S. Bureau of Labor Statistics.

and power. Throughout high-unemployment 1982, unions were compelled to negotiate contracts in autos, transportation, construction, and other industries, contracts that abandoned previous union gains. A new word, "givebacks," entered the vocabulary of labor–management bargaining.

In the new economic setting, the old question, "Are the unions too powerful?" has been opened for debate once again. The answer given to the question will have a considerable bearing on labor–management relations for a long time to come.

SYNOPSIS. The Conservative argument presents unions as true monopolists, which exact higher wages at the cost of higher prices to consumers, reduction of business profits, and interference with the labor market. The Liberal argument maintains that unions are a necessary balance to corporate power and that they have improved the general well-being of all workers. The Radical argument, while agreeing that the union movement has aided workers, holds that it has not played a sufficiently active political role and that many of organized labor's gains have come at a cost to non-union workers.

Anticipating the Arguments

- According to Conservatives, how have unions worked against the interests of workers in general?

- How do Liberals justify their claims that unions have redressed the balance of power between capital and labor?

- On what grounds do many Radicals argue that labor unions have been an essentially conservatizing force in the past?

The Conservative Argument

While union members represent only a small proportion of all American workers, unions have inordinate power. Concentrated in critical industries and trades, they are able to use extraordinary leverage in obtaining wage gains and other benefits. To a very considerable extent, their power is simple blackmail. If government or business fails to agree to union demands, the result can be devastating strikes in key industries, with spillover effects involving the entire economy. A protracted labor struggle in the steel industry, for instance, can throw millions of other Americans out of work and create a national recession. A truckers' strike can keep food off thousands of tables. With such economic strength, it is not surprising that union political power has been growing, even though membership has been more or less stabilized for the past decade.

Liberal dogma tells us that the growth of union power has been beneficial to all Americans. Does this argument stand the test of the most obvious economic analysis? How have unions produced more and more for everybody with nobody the loser? The answer is that they haven't. Union progress has had a very high pricetag for the American people.

WHO PAYS THE BILL?

First and foremost, unions adversely affect the price and total output of goods and services. Gains in wages and fringe benefits, won through union pressure, add to the costs of any firm's output. The only options for a business are to absorb the costs through lower profits or pass them on in the form of higher prices. The first alternative reduces a firm's competitive strength and lessens its ability to acquire capital and make needed investment. The second alternative penalizes consumers by forcing them to pay prices that are higher than necessary. High prices, of course, tend to stimulate higher prices, since everyone has to run a bit faster to catch up.

It is not that unions don't know about the effects of unreasonable wage gains. They don't care. I. W. Abel, former head of the United Steelworkers, was asked in 1977 whether he felt that his union's current contract demands for a guaranteed life income might not be a heavy burden for the steel industry and, ultimately, the consumer. With the unionist's typical indifference to the cost of union victories, Abel replied, "We're not concerned with that side of the question. We must look out for our members." Such an attitude contributed mightily to the decline of the American steel industry, which, by late 1982, had furloughed indefinitely more than 40 percent of its workers.

Even more burdensome than the direct wage costs of unionism are union efforts to usurp ownership and management powers. Unions force on firms contracts that interfere with efficient labor hiring and use (railroad full-crew, or "featherbedding," arrangements are an example) and that often specify maximum daily or hourly output. The result is industrial inefficiency and reduced productivity. Such violations of employers' rights to their own capital and property and their freedom to hire and fire also add to production costs and finally to consumer prices.

Furthermore, the excessive power of labor unions disrupts the operation of supply and demand in the labor market. Since unionized industries must pay higher wages, they lower their demand for labor as they shift toward greater, and cheaper, capital use. Moreover, as individuals are forced out of, or prevented from entering, jobs "protected" by unions, they drive down wage rates in other areas. With a greater supply of available labor, all things being equal, wages are lowered in non-union jobs. The overall effect of these shifts has been an increased imbalance in national income distribution. The gulf between the labor union elite and the disadvantaged bottom grows; union gains have to come from someplace, and they come mostly from other workers, especially the poorest workers.

Another undesirable effect of unionism is the aggressive advocacy of "union shop" or "agency shop" conditions for employment. Under this arrangement, a company-recognized union can compel union membership (union shop) or at least dues payment (agency shop) as a requirement for employment. Such specifications obviously deny individual workers the free choice of joining or rejecting a union. Perhaps of equal importance, this forced dues collection vastly increases a union's economic (read "strike-making") power. To halt this trend, Conservatives have fought hard in recent years for "right-to-work" laws that would end enforced union membership and union appropriation of part of each worker's pay.

Aside from these direct effects on the marketplace, others—equally undesirable—result from union efforts to develop so-called progressive legislation. A couple of examples should suffice. First, let's take union support of a national minimum wage. Superficially, this support is justified as an attempt to improve the lot of the non-union worker. In fact, unions favor the minimum wage concept because it lays an ever-rising legal floor on which they can build ever-higher union-wage ceilings. The actual result is not to help the poor but to increase union wages and lower the average non-union worker's income. This happens because hikes in the minimum wage destroy jobs, especially marginal jobs; if an employer must pay more than a worker creates in value, the employer will lay off the worker.

A second example of unions and legislation was their practice, a decade or so ago, of supporting social legislation to "protect" female workers. Protection in fact became discrimination, as laws and union contracts denied women access to certain jobs and kept them locked in low-paying "female" occupations. Feminists who charge business with sex discrimination should start looking in the right places—among the labor unions and social-rights advocates of several decades past.

One further example of excessive union influence is their use of "union-made" power. By forcing industries to purchase from and sell to unionized firms only, and by pressuring fellow unionists to buy only union-made products, industrial unions can effectively lower the demand for the goods of certain non-union firms. While this practice is a direct interference with property rights and should be opposed as such, it also creates inefficiency, destroys jobs, and causes needlessly high prices.

The unions' monopolistic efforts have a suicidal tendency. They have hurt their own members precisely as they "succeeded." Higher wages, for instance, have certainly accelerated the substitution of capital for labor. The proof is that, despite the continued growth of output in union industries, employment gains in these areas have been slight. Moreover, union wage gains have led to the export of American jobs. Competition from lower-paid workers overseas often has been the price of labor's domestic victories.

Doubters may ask, "Why should Conservatives single out union monopoly but overlook business monopoly?" The answer is simple; union monopoly is legal (exempted from antitrust laws), while business monopoly has been a crime since passage of the Sherman Anti-Trust Act. As we have argued before, government is largely responsible for monopoly creation, and government-created monopoly power is the worst kind of monopoly. Government-sanctioned labor monopoly has political as well as economic power. Situated as it is at the center of the Democratic party, the nation's majority party, labor unionism is able to entrench itself deeper and deeper politically.

THE SPECIAL PROBLEM OF PUBLIC-SECTOR UNIONISM

The political clout of the unions in recent years has been enhanced by the rapid growth of public-sector unionism. During the past twenty years, precisely as public-sector employment was undergoing rapid growth, public-sector union membership increased by over 500 percent. Today, one of every five American unionists is employed in the public sector, raising especially troublesome questions. First of all, public-sector unionism leads to unionist activity directly in opposition to the interest and welfare of the society at large. Strikes by police officers, firefighters, and teachers have become common, and the monopoly power of public-sector unions over these critical functions has led to the extortion of unjustifiably high wage increases and expensive fringe benefits (for example, pensions). Given society's dependence on the public sector, union activity in this area has produced greater relative gains for union members than has private-sector unionism. These gains are, of course, considerable tax costs to the ordinary citizen.

A second problem is that the unionizing of public employees creates a special-interest group committed to ever-expanding state bureaucracy. For instance, the 1 million members of AFSCME (American Federation of Federal, State, County and Municipal Employees) have a vested interest in protecting and expanding public-sector expenditures and areas of public intervention in the economy. The reason is obvious enough. Their jobs depend upon it. Thus, public unions can exert, through the strength of their numbers and their placement in the economy, enormous political leverage in subverting the market system. At the same time, their "gains" represent a heavy cost to the taxpayer.

DEALING WITH THE UNIONS

A Conservative program for dealing with the union problem could be reduced to the slogan "Don't outlaw the unions, outlaw their power." Workers, like everyone else, should have the right of free association. Much can be said in favor of fraternal workplace or skill organizations. Indeed, these groups should have the democratic right to lobby for their ideas and programs. However, union strength should be curtailed by a three-pronged attack on their monopoly power.

First, unions' special exemption from antitrust laws should be terminated. Second, compulsory unionism should be ended; right-to-work protection should be given all workers, whatever their feeling about joining a union. No worker should be compelled, as is now the case in many states, to join a union as a prerequisite to getting and holding a job. Third, the right to strike should be defined and limited to specific lawful ends. While workers should have the right to withhold their labor, they should not be able to do this if (1) the national welfare is endangered; (2) the purpose is purely political; (3) the union has made no effort to negotiate—in other words, no wildcat strikes; or (4) there is violence.

Such a program would go a long way toward restoring the balance of power between unions and management. With some exceptions, organized labor has marched down a one-way street for the past forty years.

With regard to the problem of public-sector unionism—its extortionist tactics and political lobbying power—there is really only one solution. As a condition of their employment public employees should be prohibited from joining unions. This is not inconsistent with, nor does it violate, a Conservative commitment to freedom and free association. It merely recognizes that government, its scale and operation, should be under the democratic control of the entire population. Public-sector unions in effect deny the general public their rights of review and control over government processes. As such they are a monopoly and special-interest infringements, on both the economic and political processes of a free society.

The Liberal Argument

The Liberal position with regard to the place of unions in the economy is very simple: Unions are necessary in order for labor to have an equitable balance with management in establishing wages, hours, and conditions of work. Without a balance of power in bargaining, one side soon dominates the other and the very essence of a pluralist democratic capitalism is endangered. From the Liberal standpoint, commitment to governmental intervention to redress imbalances is essential, for history shows that working out labor–management issues in a "free market" leads to chaos.

THE FAILURE OF FREE-LABOR BARGAINING

Contrary to the fantasies of its Conservative defenders, a free-labor market is not free at all, but controlled by the purchasers of labor. To attack unions as disrupters of the economy may be defensible within free-market logic, but it shows no understanding of economic conditions in the real world. Wiithout the protection of unions, workers have always been price-takers, forced by the necessity of survival to accept whatever wage rate is offered. To be sure, as the free-market advocate may point out, a worker is free to turn down a wage he or she considers inadequate. However, this is somewhat like saying that a person has the choice of death by poison or execution by a firing squad. Freedom there is, but the choices are equally dismal.

Perhaps in an idyllic Adam Smith world of many buyers and sellers, no one of whom had excessive economic or political power, the society might depend reasonably on the "laws of the market." At any rate, this was not the actual condition as industrial capitalism began to emerge in the last century. The few who hired had excessive power over those who worked, and unionism was a natural, humane, and necessary development. Any other view simply ignores American history.

Necessary as it was, unionism did not emerge without a long struggle. Efforts to unionize in the late nineteenth century were opposed in the courts, which upheld entrepreneurs' property rights and treated unions either as criminal conspiracies or, after the Sherman Anti-Trust Act of 1890, as monopolistic efforts to restrain trade. Management ruthlessly attempted to weed out union organizers and members. Under threat of being discharged or blacklisted, workers were compelled to sign yellow-dog contracts—promises never to join or support a union. When these efforts at intimidation were not sufficient, management simply staged lockouts—they closed down, so that laborers, without savings or strike funds, were driven back to work by the reality of starvation. When all else failed and it was faced with a full-fledged strike, management could hire strikebreakers and finally, use police and bullets.

These struggles between management and labor were creating irreversible class divisions and bloody social disorder. Haymarket, Homestead, Pullman, and Ludlow (classic labor struggles, 1880–1910) were names synonymous with industrial warfare and harbingers of what might happen on a grander scale unless labor–capital relations were improved. Largely under the pressure of Liberals, first in the Progressive Era and then during the New Deal period, a new strategy for dealing with labor–business conflicts evolved. In its simplest form, the strategy had two parts. One was legalizing and protecting the rights of workers to organize; the other was establishing the principle of collective bargaining between labor and management, in order to determine wages and work conditions in all unionized businesses. With the passage of the Wagner Act in 1935, labor received its "Magna Carta." This law forbade employer interference with workers' rights to organize unions, outlawed company unions, prohibited discriminatory antiunion action by employers, compelled employers to bargain in "good faith," and established a National Labor Relations Board to oversee labor–management affairs. Unions finally had arrived, and membership grew from 4 million in 1935 to 18 million over the next twenty years. Collective bargaining had replaced industrial violence as the basis for industry–worker relations.

It is doubtful today that many businesses would like to return to the wild "free-market" era of labor relations. Collective bargaining is as much a part of business as it is of labor. As business has grown larger and more complex, uncertainties of all kinds are less desirable. Collective bargaining and long-term labor contracts have tended to stabilize labor situations, to business's distinct pleasure. Nevertheless, criticism of unions continues. Here we must deal with several of the more inaccurate and obnoxious arguments.

CORRECTING THE EVIDENCE

Many critics of unions argue that they have caused economic inefficiency and suffering in our society. The record does not bear this out at all. Before the union movement succeeded in forcing higher wages, improved working conditions, and greater concern for the rights of labor, suffering was the common plight of *all* workers. The history books are replete with examples of the abominable working conditions during the early industrial period in England, the United States, and all developing capitalist economies. Even in the more "enlightened" modern period, union political pressures are virtually the only check to assure safe working conditions and adequate rates of pay for all workers.

Meanwhile, union-sponsored social programs in the areas of improved education, compensation for illness or disability, and security against unemployment and old age have become accepted facts of life. Without union political agitation in these areas, state and federal action simply would not have happened.

What about the charge that unions cause inefficiency, higher prices, and even joblessness? There is no hard evidence to support this claim. Although American labor struggles date back to colonial times, the great advances made by unions have come in this century, mostly in the last forty years. During this period, the United States has become the preeminent industrial power in the world. The standard of living for all Americans has advanced continually. To argue that union gains have been won at a cost to other members of society is not true. As union wages and benefits have increased, they have pulled up those of non-union workers. While unemployment and unfair income distribution remain serious problems, the modern union era—that is, 1941 to the present—has actually seen a doubling of the income share (percentage of national income) of the lowest fifth of the population. Such evidence disputes the Conservative logic that the poor pay for unionism.

With regard to the Conservative charge that union shops and agency shops deny some workers their rights and their wages by compelling them to pay union dues, Liberals view this as a smokescreen. Right-to-work laws aimed at ending this long-established practice are in reality efforts at union busting. Required union dues are designed to prevent "free riders," workers who enjoy union-gained wage and job benefits but wouldn't otherwise pay to support union expenses. Most important though, they wouldn't have these benefits and their salaries would be much lower if the comparatively small contributions to the union were not paid. It is not the worker's free choice which right-to-work advocates have in mind but the employer's. By dividing the workers against each other on the issue of union dues, worker solidarity—the first requisite for effective unionism—is destroyed. Breaking the union is the next step.

Another spurious argument used against unions is that they are the basic cause of our present rising prices through cost-push inflation. There is valid reason to believe that wage increases have occasionally been inflationary in the past—for example, in the 1950s and 1960s, when industry sometimes came to the bargaining table willing to give up more than unions were asking for. However, average real wages have fallen during most of the 1970s. Under the Carter administration's voluntary wage guidelines, labor was asked to hold the line at 7 percent annual increases, while inflation rates grew at more than 10 percent. Meanwhile, corporate profits soared, averaging more than twice the wage-rate increase during the same period. Such evidence

does not support the charge made by some cost-push critics of inflation that wage increases are the initial and causal factor in upwardly
spiraling prices.

A LIBERAL STRATEGY

Liberals' historical commitment to the cause of the union movement and concern for the rights of workers should not be uncritical, of
course. Labor's right to strike should be supported from mindless
Conservative assault; without the right to withhold their labor, workers have lost not only a democratic freedom but their most effective
tool in negotiating. But the right to strike is not absolute, to be guaranteed in all situations. Society at large has rights, too. It has the right
to military and police protection; it has the right to be spared the
physical harm that might result from certain strikes. The consistent
Liberal must look for the greater social good in such situations and not
be inflexibly committed to absolute principles.

The right to organize in the public sector poses a special problem
in balancing employee rights with those of the community. Since the
1940s, government employment has been growing faster than any
other sector of the economy, and over the past ten years union efforts
in attracting new members in the public sector have been quite successful. Most Liberals would support this growth of public-sector unionism, but not without qualifications. Indeed, do firefighters, police
officers, sanitation workers, and teachers have the right to strike in
the same sense that auto workers do? The predominant answer among
Liberals would probably be *no!*—on the grounds that such strikes often do vast and irreparable damage to the general society. For instance, President Reagan's dismissal of striking air-traffic controllers
in 1981 and the later "decertification" of their union also had considerable Liberal support. Or, at least Liberals were concerned enough
about the union's strike action not to take strong issue with the Conservative president. However, this does not mean public-sector unionism should be abolished. In New York and some other states, public
unionism is legally defined as a two-way street. Employees are required to be members of a bargaining agency (union) of their choice
but at the same time they are prohibited from striking.

While some will argue this amounts to putting discriminatory
limits on public-sector unions, they miss the point. The objective of
such legal requirements is to produce collective bargaining between

the public employer and public employee without the larger society suffering from strikes against the general welfare. Employee rights are protected through compulsory bargaining or arbitration, which makes recourse to strikes unnecessary. To be sure, public employee strikes do occur in states like New York, but not with the frequency and severity found in states that do not recognize both the employees' rights to organize to protect their interest and the society's rights to essential public services.

There may be other types of excessive union power or misuse of power, ranging from political coercion to corruption of both union and public officials. Such evils should not be overlooked simply because they are union matters. However, the Taft-Hartley Act (1947) and the Landrum-Griffin Act (1959) provide for considerable scrutiny of and control over abuses of union power. Overall, alleged abuses by organized labor can be handled without altering our commitment of the past forty years to labor–management balance.

The future, however, may hold out a new meaning for the term "balance" in labor–management relations. As we note in the next issue on productivity problems, the old adversary relationship between unions and management needs to be reshaped into a partnership. More than ever before, workers are recognizing that they have an economic stake in their place of employment, while employers are considering new "labor-participation" programs. In all this, the Japanese have been a persuasive model, illustrating that it is possible for an industrial capitalist economy to have labor peace, a reasonably compassionate approach toward workers by management, and worker involvement in decisions traditionally reserved for management. Dozens of executives and union leaders from the steel, auto, and other manufacturing industries made trips to Japan in the early 1980s to study the Japanese approach. Of course, Japanese institutions are alien to Americans, but a new union–management relationship may be adapted in America from the Japanese model. It is too early to tell yet, but many Liberals have a hunch we are on the doorstep of a brand-new era in labor–management relations.

The Radical Argument

Without much doubt, unions have brought workers protection and advantages that could not have been obtained in the "free market." By organizing together, many workers have obtained job security, higher wages, better working conditions, and a host of fringe benefits (paid vacations, retirement and health plans, and the like). These would not have been possible if they had stood, hat in hand, waiting for their capitalist employers to humanize work conditions and better their incomes.

THE FAILURES OF AMERICAN UNIONISM

There are, however, basic defects in the American system of trade unionism. First of all, with the exception of the Industrial Workers of the World (known as Wobblies) in the early twentieth century and a few communist and socialist unions of the 1930s and 1940s, American unionism usually has lacked a radical political direction. In fact, political organization or agitation of any kind has never been important in the big unions. While one thinks of the AFL-CIO and the Democratic party as almost synonymous, the union's support for this traditional party is not political activism in any radical sense. To the founding father of modern unionism, Samuel Gompers of the AFL, labor struggles were motivated basically by bread-and-butter issues. Gompers, who was interested only in organizing along craft lines, believed that unions should avoid political involvement and support the social order of capitalist society. Neither the broadening of the union movement to industrywide organizing under the CIO in the 1930s nor the AFL-CIO merger in 1955 changed this outlook. In World War I, in the New Deal of the 1930s, and in World War II, establishment unionism was rewarded handsomely by both government and business as they came to appreciate the politically nonmilitant nature of American unions. Contrary to the views of Conservatives and some Liberals, American corporate leaders came to see unions as more beneficial than detrimental. As industry, especially heavy industry, became more technically complex and economically concentrated, unions served as useful organizers of the labor supply. They provided stability in hiring and employment that more than compensated for the enforced recognition of unions and the legalization of such labor tactics as the strike, the boycott, and exclusive jurisdiction.

This is not to say that all businesses agreed with unions all the time. Some remained implacable and willing to resort to violence to destroy "bolshevik" unionism. The Republic Steel Massacre on Memorial Day 1937 is a bitter example of this type of thinking.* Such business attitudes, however, are pretty much past history, as is labor militancy. Today, few businesses oppose unions in principle, and most unions support the capitalist system in practice. Union leaders worked with the FBI and CIA in the 1950s to purge radicals from their ranks and to help eliminate radical elements in the unions of friendly foreign nations. Most union leadership vigorously supported the Vietnam War and continues to support a strong military-foreign policy for the United States. In times of domestic economic crisis, union leaders have shown a willingness to collaborate with business to hold down wages and prices, as when President Nixon introduced wage–price controls in the early 1970s. The point is that in our time, the corporate attack on unions has been mostly rhetoric; practice indicates mutual acceptance and collaboration. Not even in the deep 1982 recession did management push organized labor to the wall. "Give-backs" were obtained at the bargaining table, but no large firm turned to outright "union busting."

Although the growth of public-sector unionism often is viewed with alarm by believers in the traditional economic and political faith, it too has proved to be a blank cartridge among the weapons of working-class struggle in the United States. Very much as private-sector unions serve to organize and discipline workers in private industry, public-sector unions serve the same function in government employment. The level of militancy among public-sector workers has never proved to be very strong. During the 1950s and 1960s the general growth of the economy permitted public employee wages to rise very swiftly, in many cases faster than in the private sector. While union membership grew, it did not reflect a growing revolutionary consciousness among its members—who were, after all, doing quite well by past standards. Presently, in the wake of California's Proposition 13 and the growing fiscal crises of all governments, public-sector wage gains have slowed even below the inflation rate. However, this contraction has not produced militancy but rather passive acceptance, since many public employees frankly fear making waves as the prospect of government-sector retrenchment grows. While public employment remains extremely vulnerable during this contractionary stage in American capitalism, it

---

*Ten strikers were killed outside Chicago's Republic Steel plant on Memorial Day 1937. They were demonstrating peacefully for recognition of their union when they were fired upon and beaten by city and plant police. No police were convicted, but a number of strikers went to jail for disturbing the peace.

should be expected that unions in this sector will react no differently than other unions. They will try to protect their more senior members, even collaborating with management efforts at payroll and employment reductions if this must be the price.

RADICALS DISAGREE ON TACTICS

On labor's side, the growth of the collaboration between unions and management has been facilitated by the domination of a distant, elderly, and bureaucratic leadership. The "professional" leaders and managers of the unions usually have found themselves more at home speaking with their management counterparts than with their own members. Not infrequently, they have negotiated sweetheart contracts that sold out their members very cheaply.

Up to this point, most Radicals would agree: Labor unions have been more of a conservative than a radical force in American history, and current labor leadership is hopelessly detached from the real interests and needs of workers. But what does this mean for the future and for developing a Radical program toward labor unions?

The working class must finally be the political vehicle for radical social change. Without working-class support and, ultimately, working-class leadership, a radical reordering of society remains only the dream of intellectuals. Labor unions are a critical institution in approaching the working class, but should unions be opposed on the basis of past evidence, or should they be utilized? Radicals are divided on this question, and the division must be explained.

The anti-union position, which sometimes sounds surprisingly similar to Conservative logic, holds that unions are elitist, both at the top and among their members. Union membership is comparatively small (and even smaller than official figures indicate if we recognize that many unionists are inactive). Thus the old socialist idea of seeing the unions as a means to reach most workers is wrong today. Moreover, because of their wage and job security advantage over other workers, union members are the least politically developed of American workers. In fact, many of their wage gains have come as the result of relative wage losses (through inflation) and greater job insecurity for non-union labor. Union workers are at the top of the hierarchy of American labor, and they would have little to gain from a Radical program aimed at greater worker control of jobs and a fairer distribution of income. Arguing from these premises, some Radicals see unions as an enemy, an element that increases internal working-class warfare and division. They argue, however, that the heyday of powerful unions is over; more and more of the workforce now occupies less-secure and less-remunerative jobs. Unions thus become unnecessary and even insignificant as labor organizes directly against capital.

The other, and preponderant, Radical view argues that labor unions are essential in developing working-class consciousness against the system. To be sure, unionism is not a substitute for militant worker efforts to seize control of the means of production. However, if the present conservative leadership of unions is replaced, there is a real possibility that unions could become a progressive force toward this end. Moreover, the rank and file are increasingly militant and willing to challenge rights of management that the union leadership take for granted. Increasingly workers will move beyond mere bread-and-butter issues to deal with such questions as labor control over the introduction and use of capital equipment and labor's sharing directly in corporate earnings. Such progressive ideas and increased militancy, the pro-union argument holds, will carry over into non-union labor.

While this division among Radicals on the position of unions should not be underestimated, it is only a tactical disagreement. Organization of the working class into a radical force is still a common objective. Quite as Conservatives have stated, the Radical objective *is* to replace capitalist control with that of labor. The final goal is the social ownership of the means of production and worker determination of output. That means the bringing together of workers, union and non-union, in a common struggle and the support of all efforts to enlarge worker power, whether through existing union offices or other types of organization. Given the past history of collaboration between union bureaucracy and capitalist management, Radicals are united in their opposition to allowing elite labor leaders to act as political brokers for either their own union members or the working class as a whole. Thus, the Radical position is to go beyond the "union question" as it is posed by either Conservatives or Liberals. Radicals may differ seriously in evaluating the progressive possibilities of the existing union structure, but they agree on the necessity of organizing labor against capital in whatever ways possible.

Thus, if the real question before us is, "Are the workers too powerful?" the Radical must answer *no*. Worker power must be encouraged, either through the structure of formal unions or by other means.

ISSUE 7

Declining Productivity
Market Failure, Government Failure, or Both?

The opening up of new markets, foreign or domestic, and the organizational development from craft shop and factory to such concerns as U.S. Steel illustrate the same process of industrial mutation . . . that instantly revolutionizes the economic structure from within, instantly destroying the old one, instantly creating the new one. This process of Creative Destruction is the essential fact about capitalism. It is what capitalism consists in and what every capitalist concern has got to live with.

Joseph Schumpeter, in Capitalism, Socialism and Democracy, *1942*

Government has got to wake up to the fact that it is abusing the industrial base of this nation.

Robert E. Coleman, Riegel Textile Company, 1980

The American auto industry is a perfect example of short-term strategic planning by American business.

Donald W. Mitchell, Business Consultant, 1981

I came to work Monday morning and they said they were closing the plant after the last shift on Thursday. I got a car and a house to pay for. I don't know what I'm going to do.

Out of Work, Muncie, Indiana, 1982

THE PROBLEM

In general, economists view economic growth as a macroeconomic problem—an assessment of the entire economy's output performance. However, the economic growth of nations invariably depend upon the productivity of the country in question, and productivity—the ratio of output to input—remains an essentially microeconomic matter, focusing on how businesses hire and use capital, labor, and other resource inputs in their output of goods and services.

The interconnectedness of national economic growth and productivity is apparent if we look at the American case. What we find is two disturbing trends. As Table 7.1 indicates, the long-term growth trend of the United States, until recently, has compared quite well with other noncommunist industrial nations. Only Japan exceeded our performance over the 100 years after 1870, and that mostly reflected the abysmal poverty position from which the Japanese started. However, over the past two decades, all the industrial economies except the United Kingdom have exceeded our performance. Worse still, if we focused only on the years since 1970, we have averaged less than a 3-percent growth rate. The downward trend in growth, of course, means each of us on the average can expect smaller annual improvements in our standard of living.

Table 7.1   Growth of Real GNP and Real GNP Per Capita in Selected Countries, 1870–1977

	Growth Rates of Real GNP (%)		Growth Rates of Real GNP per capita (%)	
	1870–1969	1960–1977	1870–1969	1960–1977
United States	3.7	3.6	2.0	2.4
Japan	4.2	8.7	—	7.4
Germany	3.0	3.8	1.9	3.2
United Kingdom	1.9	2.4	1.3	2.1
France	2.0	4.9	1.7	4.0
Italy	2.2	4.4	1.5	3.7
Canada	3.6	5.1	1.8	3.4

Source: U.S. Department of Commerce, *Historical Statistics of the United States, Colonial Times to 1970* (Washington, 1975), p. 225; and *Statistical Abstract of the United States, 1979*, p. 437, as cited in Campbell R. McConnell, *Economics: Principles and Problems* (New York: McGraw-Hill, 1981) p. 393.

Figure 7.1 shows the underlying cause of America's declining growth and our sagging production performance compared to other nations. American productivity, quite simply, is in a nosedive. Although other nations' productivity rates also have fallen in recent years, they remain superior to ours. With greater output in comparison to similar inputs, these nations are successfully challenging American industry in world markets, as well as in our own back yard.

Although output per hour of labor is the usual basis for measuring productivity, it is obvious that the American productivity problem goes much deeper than the question of how hard the individual American works. After all, workers can be *more* or *less* productive if they have *more* or *less* capital goods (machinery) to work with. An hour of work done by a person with a pick and shovel will not challenge the output of an individual with a backhoe. All of this leads to another dimension of the problem: Is the capital being used, even if it is of great quantity, at the highest level of available technology? Then, of course, we might ask: Is the available technology the best we are capable of producing? Overarching all these

FIGURE 7.1   HOW U.S. PRODUCTIVITY LAGS IN MANUFACTURING*

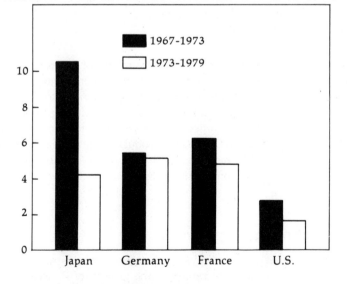

*Average compounded annual percent increase
Source: U.S. Bureau of Labor Statistics, 1980.

components of productivity is the question of management skill: Is American industry managed in an intelligent and efficient way so as to assure the best decisions about what is produced, how much of it, and under what production arrangements?

The evidence, or course, suggests that somewhere, perhaps everywhere, in the labyrinth of economic forces that determine productivity, something is wrong. Depending upon ideological viewpoint, there is a long list of possible culprits: government intervention, excessively powerful unions, poor business decision making, the "quick profit" motive, too much business dependence on government, a decline in entrepreneurship, and so on. The differing assessments of the causes and possible cures for flagging American productivity go to the very roots of the ideological differences among our economic paradigms. Yet there is something each can agree upon: America faces a serious productivity problem that must be resolved. While each ideological view may follow a different path, all could agree (for different reasons, of course) with the *Business Week* editors' conclusion that "to rebuild America's productive capacity ... will require sweeping changes in basic institutions, in the framework of economic policy making, and in the way the major actors on the scene—business, labor, and government—think about what they put into the economy and what they get out."

SYNOPSIS. To Conservatives, the recent tumbling of American productivity is directly traceable to government intervention in business decision making and the growing American desire to receive more for less work. Liberals see the productivity problem as basically resulting from inadequate business policies, in particular the short-term profit focus of most enterprises. Radicals argue that worker productivity in fact has remained quite high among most American industries and that it is not really productivity but profits that concern most business leaders.

Anticipating the Arguments

- In what specific ways do Conservatives see government economic activity retarding the growth of American productivity?

- What particular elements of recent business activity or inactivity do Liberals see as major contributions to the declining rate of American output?

- How do Radicals prove their contention that profit making, not productivity, is the real driving force in private enterprise?

The Conservative Argument

Frequently the decline of American productivity is approached as if it were the root of our economic problems. Such a perspective is mistaken; falling productivity is the result of our economic problems, many of which we have addressed already in these pages. To be blunt and direct, low productivity is the price an economic and social system must pay when it ceases to be organized solely to satisfy the objectives of profit making. As we have pointed out earlier in discussions of agricultural pricing, consumer product-safety efforts, energy policy making, antitrust policy, and business regulation, the political and economic impulse to "improve upon the market" has been virtually irresistible over the past fifty years. These interferences with the market, however, have had a very simple and, if honestly considered, obvious effect: We systematically have shifted resources and concerns out of productive sectors of the economy into nonproductive sectors. The result has been to stifle initiative and efficiency and to encourage waste and economic decline.

THE ROLE OF GOVERNMENT TAX AND SPENDING POLICIES

Government's role in reducing productivity can be categorized into at least two general areas of incorrect actions: (1) the actual physical expansion of the government's claim on the nation's output and (2) the various interventions of government into resource markets, social policy making, and pricing decisions that affect the activities of what remains of the private sector.

The growth of government's share of the Gross National Product from a mere 7 percent in 1902 to more than one third today is not simply a matter of cutting up the total economic pie in different proportions. To follow the analogy, the aggregate growth of government activities has altered the recipe of the pie and interfered with the cook's ability to bake it. The growth of a government's budget, of course, has two sides—revenues and expenditures. Each must be examined separately to see how government interferes in microeconomic decision making.

Revenues   First of all, the immense taxation necessary to sustain the government sector interferes directly with the industrial production and allocation decisions of enterprises. There is simply no such thing as a neutral tax policy. Worse still, even if some tax policies were less biased than others, American tax programs of the past fifty years have been constructed purposely by Liberal social engineers *not* to have unbiased affects. Taxes have been used for many other things than just collecting revenues to finance bloated budgets. In particular, taxes have been used as tools to redistribute income, converting the earnings of the more productive members of the society into outright gifts to the least productive. While we will explore this problem in the next issue, it should be noted that such penalizing of the productive elements of a nation and rewarding the nonproductive gives precisely the wrong signals in a society worried about improving productivity.

The decision to tax upper-income groups very heavily is among the most dangerous of Liberal aberrations. The usual economic justification for higher taxes on upper incomes is that they are relatively "painless," falling on individuals who have a diminishing value (marginal utility) for each additional dollar received. However, the national economic effects are not painless. Such taxation reduces the nation's fund of savings, which is mostly supplied by the well-to-do. Savings are, of course, the source for investment funds; therefore, reductions in the nation's savings limits the ability of business to expand and it ultimately lowers productivity. Only in recent years, with the growing understanding of "supply-side economics" has this obvious but long-overlooked result of our tax policies been given much consideration. However, recognition is one thing and changing policy direction another. The need for policy redirection is evident in Figure 7.2, which shows American investment rates shrinking compared with other industrialized countries.

Complementing our foolish personal income tax policies is our corporate tax system. Again, our search for a neutral and painless tax

FIGURE 7.2 THE SHORTFALL IN U.S. SAVING AND INVESTMENT*

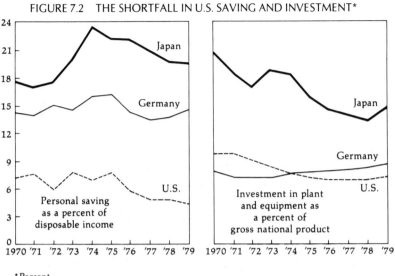

*Percent

Source: Business Week, June 30, 1980, p. 61.

has led us to grief. Taking nearly half of all corporations' net earnings in tax revenues is scarcely neutral and can only restrict an enterprise's ability to make new capital investment. Corporate taxation policies, apart from robbing firms of necessary capital resources, have other undesirable effects. By taxing profits, losses actually become less of a problem. In some cases, profit-making firms actually seek to acquire losers. After all, an approximately 50-percent corporate profits tax also means a subsidy of 50¢ on the dollar for any losses incurred in operations. While the long-run effect of operating a firm at a loss is obviously bankruptcy, the creative accounting encouraged by our corporate profits tax produces substantial short-run benefits to a firm's income statement and balance sheet. Yet, the short-run advantages are still a matter of subsidizing inefficiency. Firms and industries that should be allowed, even encouraged, to be swallowed up by what Joseph Schumpeter called capitalism's "gales of creative destruction" are kept alive for tax purposes.

Not all tax policies have unintended negative effects on productivity. Some tax policies are created consciously to discourage efficient business decision making. The best example is the long-time AFL-

CIO/Liberal effort to contain the investment of American firms within the United States by placing prohibitive taxes on multinational businesses. Reformers argue that productivity and employment are falling in the United States because some American firms are able to obtain better returns on their capital overseas. So-called "runaway firms" supposedly are starving their domestic production facilities on purpose. Never mind that unions, through outrageous labor agreements, have priced American workers out of world labor markets and placed important restrictions on the ability of business to innovate and introduce new capital-intensive production methods. Never mind that practically the only American corporations to show steady improvement in earnings and productivity are the very ones that have exploited multinational investment, production, and sales. We are asked to disregard all this and to tax the efficient firm so it will stay home and remain inefficient.

To recapitulate, under current government tax policies, capital and technology sources for productivity growth are made scarce. At the same time, corporations are discouraged by tax policy from acting wisely as profit managers. Instead of heeding the market command to close down unproductive operations, tax policies gentle and hide the market signal.

Expenditures   On the expenditures side of government operations, the shift of resources from productive to unproductive agents is even stronger. The social expenditures made in the name of a better life for "working Americans"—everything from welfare to unemployment insurance to Social Security—have the ironic effect of discouraging work altogether (more on this in the next issue). With greater numbers of the labor force artificially insulated from the market forces of supply and demand, the desire to work, and especially the desire to work very hard, is deeply eroded. Nonwork, after all, is to be rewarded and no one can slip through the "safety net," however hard they try.

From the point of view of productivity, this situation, along with the excessive power of labor unions to write their own work rules, means that labor inputs in production are vastly changed from earlier presafety-net and pre-union days. Quite simply, we all have become accustomed to working less diligently. The decline of the "work ethic" is of course not all bad. Few Conservatives will defend the 72-hour week and the intolerable working conditions of a century ago. But we cannot have it both ways. Increased productivity has made possible better hours and better wages; however, better hours and better wages are not possible in the future unless our output increases. If we choose to work less while at the same time we are producing less, then we must accept living on less. There is no such thing as a free lunch.

Lowered worker productivity is not the only outcome of government spending programs. Transfers to undeserving corporations, such as Chrysler, and subsidies to nonproducers similarly are a method of taxing the productive sectors of the economy to benefit the unproductive. They are not "free rides," but entail a cost we all must pay.

THE ROLE OF GOVERNMENT SOCIAL POLICY

Apart from budgetary actions, government also has reduced productivity by its direct intervention in business affairs through misguided social policies. The list of such offenses against market efficiency is virtually limitless, and we have discussed several in earlier issues, so a few cases must serve to point out the problem.

Environmental protection remains very high among the American people's priorities. As social objectives, clean air, water, and earth, and conservation of resources for future generations are certainly noble concerns. Indeed, environmental protection can be had without abandoning the market system—if we understand it is not a free good and are willing to pay the price. Trouble arises when we believe there are no costs or when we fail to calculate the costs accurately. In terms of the productivity problem, our noncalculation of environmental costs and our failure to assign these costs in some rational manner to consumers of goods has had the effect of undermining the ability of American enterprise to produce efficiently. The Environmental Protection Agency's overly zealous efforts in the 1970s to end industrial pollution caused many firms to take actions that limited their productive ability. Capital investment required to meet EPA emissions controls reduced the amount of capital available for new investment and for research and development. Some production operations were closed altogether when business enterprises determined that cleanup costs exceeded profit possibilities. The air got cleaner in many American industrial cities during the 1970s precisely as the lines at the unemployment office grew longer. By singling out business as the cause of the environmental problems and by placing heavy cleanup burdens upon business enterprise, we traded off jobs and productivity for a cleaner but very expensive environment. While actual job losses are difficult to estimate, *Forbes* magazine calculates that meeting government environmental standards between 1972 and 1977 caused from 500 to 1000 plant closings and lowered productivity by 1.3 percent.

Similarly, the two-decade struggle to end racial discrimination through certain economic contrivances has not uplifted many minorities or female workers, but it has raised the cost of government administration and created at the upper levels of employment a "reverse discrimination" hiring effect. Those who condemn a free economy's inability to absorb minorities and women quickly into mainstream employment fail to understand the problem. Most workers who are allegedly "discriminated against" do not in a real economic sense deserve, here and now, to be in the mainstream. Only in the simple-minded thinking of Liberals and Radicals does it make economic sense to promote unqualified and inexperienced workers and upper-level managers, over more productive "mainstream" employees. While many white males may rejoice at such an observation, they should not misunderstand it. Claims to jobs or to promotions depend solely upon one's efficiency and diligence. If any other criteria are used, then both reason and order cease to exist in labor markets; and as labor market disorder grows, output shrinks.

It should be obvious that the list of recent social engineering efforts that lower output and raise costs goes on and on. It also should be obvious that none of these efforts, however well intended, will succeed if the nation is unable to increase productivity.

THE PROBLEM OF CHOICES AND EXPECTATIONS

The productivity enigma points up a fundamental economic principle (really *the* fundamental economic principle) that always is taught rigorously in economics courses but is forgotten so easily in ordinary life: *opportunity cost.* Everything, absolutely everything this side of the land of the tooth fairy, costs something. The decline of American productivity is not the result of some twist of fate. It is not caused by the Japanese or the Germans or even the Russians. It is not, as too many believe, unexplainable. Our lowered productivity is the result of our decisions, collectively and individually, to opt for more nonoutput. Rarely does the decision present itself this way, but that is exactly what we are choosing when we choose clean air over industrial smoke, affirmative action over free-labor markets, a subsidized early retirement over work, keeping Chyrsler alive rather than letting it fall into bankruptcy, taxing the rich heavily to sustain the nonrich, and so on.

From a Conservative point of view, many of the nonoutput decisions are defensible, so long as everyone agrees to the objectives and understands that the result will be a lowered standard of living. However, most of our nonoutput decisions are imposed by the few on the many. That is pure tyranny—not democratically defensible on any grounds. Philosophically, it is wrong. Economically, it is disastrous. Unless we realize soon that our unrealistic expectations about the "good life" for everyone (deserving or not) and our reliance upon government to painlessly fulfill these expectations only produce the opposite of the intended effects, productivity declines will continue. And as the economic pie shrinks and expectations stay the same or rise, the economic truths of the market will be superseded by the reality of raw political power and force. In such a world, freedom, individualism, and democracy have ceased; and economists, already hard pressed to explain what principles guide their thinking, will simply be trotted out to bless whatever particular tyranny is in authority.

The Conservative scenario for improving productivity is, by this point in the text, self-evident: Rely on the market forces to organize and direct production. Artificial interventions by Liberal social tinkerers, by manipulative labor unions, and by well-organized minority issue groups prohibit market efficiency. They shift investment in and rewards to the unproductive elements and activities of the society. The market cannot resolve instantaneously all of the social problems, real and alleged, that exist. But in the long run, as the illustrious past record of American productivity and growth shows, the market will decide the *what, how,* and *for whom* questions much more efficiently than can government or some weird mixture of government and the market.

Declining productivity is the result of a failure of the market produced by the failure of government. The continued decline of productivity will produce the failure of everything that we hold of value. Without continued growth, we all must have less, which we are not prepared by our nature to accept. This paradox is the central economic and political fact of our time. It will be solved one way or another, for better or ill.

The Liberal Argument

Contrary to the Conservative view that the downward trend in American productivity is traceable to government interference in the market, the problem largely results from the failure of one factor of production which Conservatives seem to take as a given: entrepreneurship, or management. Among the enlightened business observers of the problem, who are now calling for a "reindustrialization" of America, comparatively few have picked government as the sole cause of our industrial troubles. Instead, most thoughtful business leaders shun the narrow Conservative view and agree with Thomas Murphy, Chairman of General Motors Corporation, who has observed: "The 1970s were all but a disaster . . . we seem to have spent our time not making decisions but postponing them." As a result, Murphy and other business leaders conclude that the rebuilding of American industry will be possible only through greater long-term planning efforts—by corporations, government, and the representatives of labor. That is a far cry from appealing to a return to the unregulated market.

THE PROBLEM OF FALTERING CORPORATE STRATEGIES

In his *New Industrial State*, John Kenneth Galbraith argued almost twenty years ago that planning has taken on a central role in the modern giant corporation. Not to plan, to leave business decisions to the short-term whims of the market, was simply too irresponsible a business strategy to contemplate. While Galbraith doubtless was correct in his observation, his timing was wrong, for American enterprise had not yet reached the level of mature corporate planning. Now confronted with falling productivity, tumbling profits, and dwindling shares of both domestic and world markets, long-term corporate planning may be coming of age.

Looking back over the past decade's decline in American productivity, the shallowness of business strategy becomes apparent. In the first place, preoccupation with short-term profits by most firms led to neglecting long-term trends and to adjusting corporate strategy to them. Nowhere was this more obvious than the auto industry. After the energy shortage of 1973, the market (even as Conservatives understand "market") gave clear signals that the era of the 300-HP Dinosaur Eights was over. However, as buyers began to sample Japanese and German "world cars" in greater numbers, Detroit continued to follow the old tried-and-true strategy of the auto industry: Make them big and fast! As a result, American auto dealers' lots continued to fill up in the mid and late 1970s with unsold giant machines while the roads became cluttered with more VWs, Datsuns, Toyotas, and Hondas. Within five years of the energy crisis, Detroit lost 20 percent of the American car market to foreigners. Worse still, the auto giants were slow to use their enormous capital resources to design and build the kind of cars that energy prices forced Americans to buy. When the changes finally came in the late 1970s, they were done swiftly, creating serious design, production, and marketing problems. Helped along by the recession, 1981 Detroit sales were only a little more than half those of the golden years of the late 1960s.

Corporate policy in the 1970s also reflected a short-term profit bias. Giant firms followed an essentially foolish merger process. The then-popular corporate myth that sheer size was a measure of strength led to thousands of ill-conceived combinations. Established and efficient giants squandered their cash and credit acquiring enterprises in wholly unrelated industries. In 1981, more than $80 billion was spent on corporate acquisitions. This was more than all American firms spent on research and development. None of the acquisitions created new value—they only reorganized the corporate ownership landscape. Meanwhile, firms grew larger but they grew weaker as capital resources were overextended and management and marketing problems developed in the new, unfamiliar operations that had been acquired.

The short-term strategy of quick growth through takeover was paced by another trend in dangerous short-term planning: multinational growth. From most firms' perspectives, multinational operations made sense; and looked at solely from the firm's balance sheet, they still do. The lure of cheaper overseas labor markets and the possibility of tapping enormous overseas final-goods markets was irresistible. By 1980, firms like IBM were earning 50 percent of their profits in overseas operations. Of course, much of this flight of capital overseas was helped along by government tax policy, which virtually left overseas earnings untaxed. However, the short-term profitability and even the long-term profitability of overseas operations often added up to declining profits at home. Each investment dollar going overseas was a dollar not invested in improving domestic production facilities. Plants in the United States grew old and obsolete as new structures went up in France, Italy, Brazil, Formosa, and Germany. Steel, once the backbone of American industry, limped along in the United States, using turn-of-the-century plants and production methods. The effects, of course, were low productivity and high costs.

Meanwhile, as American business squandered its technological, management, and production leadership through short-term profit strategies, other industrial nations, particularly Japan and Germany, took a long-run view. Through coordinated capital planning, along with supportive government actions, their productivity soon surpassed the United States'. By the early 1980s, both Japan and Germany had almost caught up to the United States in output per worker. Meanwhile, the United States, once the world leader in standard of living, had fallen to tenth in the world.

Far from the Conservative scenario of a shrinking economic pie caused by workers opting for less labor and more leisure and a government hamstringing industry with taxes and social-legislation requirements, we find the American economic pie has been getting smaller because the corporate cook has been skimping on capital and management skills, two key ingredients of growth.

THE NECESSITY FOR DEVELOPING A NEW GOVERNMENT ROLE

Despite the fact that corporate America may have caused the productivity crisis, the problem is too large for it to solve by itself. "Reindustrialization" requires new government policies to promote productivity improvements. Given the modernization needs of American industry (it is estimated $150 billion in investment is needed to bring the nation's industry up to date) and the tendency of enterprises to waste their capital on acquisitions or to send it overseas, a massive business-assistance and capital-planning program is needed.

In the area of assisting business development, both representatives of business and labor have called for creating a "temporary national economic commission," made up of representatives of industry, labor, government, and academia. Felix Rohatyn, a former ITT executive and a partner of the Lazard Frères Investment House (hardly a man of Radical background), has described the commission's role as devising "an industrial strategy which, coupled with tax policy, would have its objective to reverse the decline of the manufacturing sector." One of Rohatyn's pet projects, and an idea gaining broader Liberal support, is the establishment of a federal investment fund, patterned after the old Reconstruction Finance Corporation of the Great Depression years. The object of the fund would be to make low-interest, long-term loans to financially troubled corporations—firms that otherwise might not secure needed funds in private markets and thereby might fail.

Another assistance project, widely supported by business but opposed by Conservatives, is to increase investment in human capital. By developing job-training programs and paying subsidies to businesses that hire the poorly skilled, this type of government outlay would work in two ways to increase national output: Welfare (nonproductive) payments would be reduced *and* worker productivity would be raised.

To halt the squandering of capital funds in productively pointless and wasteful mergers and to shift such monies toward actual reinvestment in capital facilities, a new corporate tax policy must be considered. By using a mix of tax reductions on new productive investment and tax penalties on mergers that do not demonstrate possible economies of scale, an effective "carrot-and-stick" approach to better investment strategy would emerge. Similarly, such a discretionary tax policy could be employed to slow down the rate of capital flight into multinational corporations' overseas operations. Presently many firms find that their overseas tax payments are deductible against their U.S. tax liabilities; thus, tax policy tends to encourage migration of capital. By removing such privileges and by placing other tax restraints upon the firm, tax policy could be used to encourage corporate "deepening" of investment in the United States. Meanwhile, the careful and selective use of tariffs and import quotas can provide breathing space for industries presently hard pressed by foreign competition. The "free-trade" argument of Conservatives, however convincing the logic, will not give American enterprise the time it needs to reindustrialize.

Of course, there remains the broader question of just what we should be investing our national capital in. Obviously a scattergun approach that provides a little capital for everyone will not be as effective as directing large amounts of resources to areas where we have a particular advantage. Moreover, our investment needs are far greater in the area of capital goods production than in quality-of-life improvements. To be direct, it is a lot more important that the American steel industry be redeveloped than that McDonald's be able to renovate its golden arches. Necessarily, this involves choices—*indicative planning*—by government or a quasigovernmental agency such as the proposed temporary national economic planning commission.

Another necessary line of policy by government is to stimulate savings and reduce consumption. Despite Conservative arguments that voluntary savings/consumption decisions work best, the evidence does not support the claim. Americans of all income levels have become accustomed to high mass consumption. Savings at all levels of income have fallen. Forced savings through consumption taxes, such as value-added taxes, offer about the only short-term means to reverse this trend.

Such programs as we have outlined here will increase the availability of capital resources. By broadening and deepening our capital base, we can start to reverse the productivity decline, yet capital shortage and wasteful investment is not the only problem.

A NEW PARTNERSHIP BETWEEN BUSINESS AND LABOR

Regardless of our capital strength, labor remains the chief component in all productivity questions. In this area, reindustrialization requires new approaches to labor–management relations. In particular, the traditional adversary relationship between workers and employers must end. Neither the old capitalist mentality of complete control over workers nor the unionist approach of "more, more, more" can be permitted if reindustrialization is to succeed. Both capital and labor can learn much from the Japanese model. There, earnings (wages and shared profits) are tied to increased productivity. Workers as well as management have a shared interest in the outcome of the firm's operations; however, labor is not a passive element, simply accepting management decisions and sharing in their effects. On the contrary, labor, right down to the least significant employee on the plant floor, participates in a variety of management decisions. Labor input is not limited to such matters as wages and hours but is involved in how goods are manufactured, how jobs are defined, where responsibility lies, and so on.

Such a change in industrial relations is not a cosmetic change at all. Effectively, it redefines the power balance between labor and capital. It admits that the modern corporation is not manageable from remote corporate offices. The era of the old enterprise is over. Meanwhile, a highly structured staff of professional managers also has proven unable to handle the complexities of a modern corporation. Only by sharing management and labor decision-making will corporations be able to adapt to the new production requirements. Conservatives who hold out for the traditional powers of corporate leadership and a passive, dominated role for labor are still living in the era of Adam Smith's pin factory. They fail to understand that the complexity and interconnectedness of production today require more than division of labor. There must be shared responsibility. They also fail to comprehend that we are at the end of the era of individual, atomistic workers and capitalists, each doing their selfish materialist thing. Probably no aspect of the reindustrialization process is so potentially revolutionary in changing economic and social relations in modern mixed capitalism as the changes that must take place in the workplace. Economics as it is known and taught in the United States has yet to absorb these trends into conventional theory.

A SUMMING UP

Closing the productivity gap, quite as Conservatives argue, is essential for the nation to survive and for the production-for-profit system to continue. However, by maintaining and defending a no-government, no-labor-union, no-social-policy approach to all output decisions, Conservatives, even if they succeeded in generating greater productivity and economic growth, would limit the benefits to a very few in the society. For most of us, growth or no growth would make little difference. Unless everyone shares in a rising productivity, the social and political foundations of our society will collapse and the productivity question itself will become as irrelevant as debating how many angels are able to dance on the head of a pin.

The Radical Argument

Conservative and Liberal handwringing over U.S. industrial output is deceptive. Discussion tends to focus only on one aspect of the problem. While productivity may indeed measure the relative output capacity of a nation, it is not, in a capitalist society, the measure of economic performance Conservatives and Liberals suggest it is. Profits, not productivity, are the guide for capitalist decision making and only in the obscurantist models of advanced microeconomics do the two become the same thing. In the real world, businesspeople know the difference, and they always follow profits. As Thorstein Veblen argued long ago, the businessperson's desire for profitable buying and selling very often leads to wasteful production. However, business ". . . makes up for its wastefulness by the added strain which it throws upon those engaged in the production work." In our time, the search for profits has meant declining national productivity *and* increased worker exploitation and anguish.

UNRAVELING THE DECLINING PRODUCTIVITY PARADOX

The problem of declining national productivity needs to be clarified. Both the Conservative and Liberal scenarios somehow suggest that for one reason or another—too much government interference or too little management initiative—capitalists have stopped acting like capitalists. That is, their arguments suggest business has stopped introducing labor-saving devices. In fact, the evidence is quite to the contrary. Productivity—output per worker—remains high and is rising in many sectors of the economy. In the manufacturing sector it has become spectacular. To take some representative firms for example, between 1964 and 1980, the real value of each worker's output increased 40 percent at General Motors, 90 percent at U.S. Steel, and 45 percent at IBM. In fact, in 1980 U.S. Steel produced almost twice the 1964 output with 40,000 less workers.

The low overall productivity rates develop when we add in the labor that has been squeezed from high-productivity sectors of the economy, such as manufacturing, and has been forced into less-productive (and less-rewarded) service industry and government work, or into unwanted idleness. Even in the highly productive manufacturing sector, output-per-worker averages are reduced artificially by adding in the employment of growing numbers of nonproductive managerial, promotional, and office personnel. It must be remembered that the national productivity rate is a ratio of the entire labor force to the levels of national output. In America, there has been a steady growth of marginally productive and nonproductive labor since the late 1950s. This development is not accidental, nor is it evidence that capitalists have forgotten how to use labor to their advantage. Rather, it simply reflects a new stage in our economic development.

The decline in overall productivity has not produced corporate profit declines; indeed, before-tax profit rates have stayed very steady (except in recession years) over the past several decades. The reason for this is that productivity is only one element affecting profits. The other major constraint on profit making is the labor wage rate. Wage rates are an industrial firm's real guide to how "productive" labor is. After all, what does management care about "output per hour?" The firm isn't spending *hours*. Firms spend dollars to obtain hours. Thus, output per wage dollar is the "productivity" measure that really counts.

In the earlier epochs of industrial development, productivity gains allowed for the advance of profits and for the gradual improvement of real wages. In recent years, a new trend has developed. Looking at the whole economy, maintaining stable profit rates has entailed both limiting productivity advances (at least in the leading industrial sectors) and holding down real wage rates where possible (usually in the least-productive sectors). In other words, with average productivity gains falling for the entire economy, profits increasingly were obtained by reducing average real wages. Interestingly enough, the past decade's falling national productivity has been paced by a 7.6-percent decline in the average worker's real wages over the same period.

In terms of particular corporate strategies used to force wages down and profits up, two developments are illustrative of the problem facing American workers: capital flight overseas and "runaway" firms at home.

THE INTERNATIONALIZATION OF CAPITAL

Falling American productivity began at almost precisely the same time that American enterprises began to discover the advantages of multinational operations and investment. The increasing shift of American capital to overseas production, beginning in the mid 1950s, accelerated the already evident trend of a growing labor surplus in the American economy. Almost exactly when American firms expanded overseas, unemployment began to rise and real wages began to stagnate. Only the war economy of the Vietnam era masked the seriousness of this exporting of employment.

The newest and best American technology rushed overseas to fill the new European markets for electronics, machine tools, and consumer goods. Cheap foreign skilled labor attracted other investment to the Far East, where goods were produced for sale in the United States. The effect of both moves was virtually to halt the growth of skilled jobs in the United States. At the same time, labor-intensive firms discovered the unskilled labor markets of Korea, Taiwan, and the Philippines, where workers were paid the equivalent of 20¢ an hour. This discovery had adverse effects on unskilled American labor. Only the domestic growth of low-wage jobs in the service sector and the expansion of government war and social spending mitigated the dramatic export of employment. It does not demand mastery of *Das Capital* to realize that an economy based on McDonald's drive-ins, war, and government bureaucracies is in deep trouble.

The reported profits of multinational corporations (MNCs), which are certainly much lower than their real profits, expanded precisely as the well-being of most Americans declined. Income inequality was increased, government fiscal problems worsened, and labor's bargaining power diminished. The MNC export of domestic capital (past American labor) was producing a tremendous economic contraction in America. By the mid 1970s, Americans everywhere were being urged to lower their expectations as workers and consumers. Corporations, however, were not lowering their profit targets. From an American point of view, the MNC was an effective new tool of capitalist exploitation at home.

RUNAWAY FIRMS AT HOME

As we have noted, the flight of capital overseas did not prevent some important productivity gains in domestic industry, but one can only speculate on what these gains might have been had not the cheaper overseas wage rates drawn off billions of investment dollars.

Nevertheless, overseas investment began to trigger a "disinvestment" process at home. With many firms putting their best resources overseas, their domestic plants began to decay. At the same time, labor surpluses began to grow. This encouraged the new domestic strategy of runaway plants—running not always overseas but often to new, lower-cost, (read: "lower-wage") areas within the United States. In particular, industry found the unorganized labor markets of the southern states to their liking. During the 1970s, the "frostbelt" lost 111 jobs for every one hundred that were created, while the "sunbelt" lost eighty for every one hundred new jobs. The result was industrial devastation across the Northeast and Midwest and a miniboom in the South. While many of the new plants used the best and newest technology, some firms found the labor-wage differential so attractive that many smaller industries avoided capital-intensive production methods, choosing instead inefficient but profitable labor-intensive techniques.

The domestic runaway firm leaves more than its own wreckage in its wake. The effect on the local community is not merely the jobs lost by the initial closing. There follows a "multiplier" contraction effect as services and businesses supported by the industry or the paychecks of its workers shrivel up after the initial closing. Indeed, other businesses, especially small enterprises, also then may be candidates for failure. With a growing reduction of production and jobs, the community is hit by declining revenues on one side of its budget and rising social expenditures to support unemployed workers on the other. Taxes rise and costs rise for other firms, encouraging additional closings. Meanwhile, the local pool of unemployed grows, reducing union bargaining power and reducing non-union wage rates.

TOWARD THE SOCIAL PLANNING OF PRODUCTION

Viewing the so-called productivity crisis this way, we see that efforts at lowered output costs and greater profits have a paradoxical result. While the individual enterprise acts rationally to ensure its own survival, the entire society is decimated. Individual firms may prosper, but only by driving down the general level of the nation's well-being. Obviously, Conservative efforts to end the few existing restraints on business behavior and to free up the profit effort can lead only to an acceleration of these tendencies. Despite the passing popularity of Conservative ideology, the unspeakable social and private anguish that would result from applying their programs is generally appreciated by most business and political leaders. Most people correctly understand that that kind of business freedom would quickly destroy social and political order and the production-for-profit system altogether.

Consequently, the Liberal program for a shared business–government planning of "reindustrialization" reflects a much more realistic effort by capitalists, at least temporarily, to save themselves and their system. From a Radical perspective, it is easy to point out the contradictions of such an effort—for instance, building up capitalist power on the one hand while sharing its authority with workers on the other. Yet, over the short run, such a strategy is indeed a likely alternative; and, from a Radical perspective, it is not altogether objectionable—*in the short run*. The Liberal recognition of the need to restrain and redirect individual corporate behavior and of the need to create a new relationship between capital and labor in fact could mean the beginning of social control over capital. Workers and consumers, of course, soon will learn to expect and then to demand more control than Liberals are willing to give; but the modern reformers of the production-for-profit system will not be able to withstand this pressure, and greater social control will result.

Whether or not this scenario develops very quickly remains to be seen. What is obvious in the current productivity decline, however, is the fact that one era of American business expansion, in which both business profits and worker's earnings advanced, has now ended. Real corporate growth presently means greater real losses to people. The need for social control over the basic economic questions of what is produced, how, and for whom, becomes more evident as the capitalist answer to these questions becomes increasingly unacceptable in human terms.

ISSUE 8

Problems of Income Distribution
Can Poverty Be Cured?

Like all other contracts, wages should be left to the fair and free competition of the market, and should never be controlled by the interference of the legislature.

    The clear and direct tendency of the poor laws is in direct opposition to those obvious principles: it is not as the legislature benevolently intended, to amend the condition of the poor, but to deteriorate the condition of both poor and rich; instead of making the poor rich, they are calculated to make the rich poor.

David Ricardo, 1821

It is not to die, or even to die of hunger, that makes a man wretched; many men have died, all men must die. . . . But it is to live miserable we know not why; to work sore and yet gain nothing; to be heart-worn, weary yet isolated, unrelated, girt in with a cold, universal Laissez Faire.

Thomas Carlyle, 1853

. . . a very substantial portion of poverty and unemployment is chronic, beyond the control of individuals or the influence of rising aggregate demand.

The President's Commission on
Income Maintenance Programs, 1969

THE PROBLEM

In the early 1960s, while the nation enjoyed an unprecedented level of general affluence, an annoying and irreverent little book gained a growing audience, Michael Harrington's *Other America* announced the "discovery" of an entire subculture of poverty in the United States. It proclaimed that poverty existed among the black of the inner cities, among the elderly and ill, and in the worn-out farming areas of the nation. Moreover, these poor were "invisible," hidden away from the sight of an affluent suburban majority. Looking back now, more than two decades later, Harrington's discovery of poverty should not have been nearly as surprising as it then seemed, nor should it have caused the political and economic fallout that eventually developed. Almost any thoughtful person knew that poverty had existed long before *The Other America* and Presidents Kennedy and Johnson put the matter high on the nation's social agenda. When Lyndon Johnson announced in 1964 that the federal government would wage a "War on Poverty," however, a new political mythology about ending poverty in the United States was created.

In the past the poor had been largely neglected. Suddenly they were thrust to center stage. Publishers of economics textbooks quickly added brand-new chapters on poverty and income distribution. Politicians paid lip service, at least at election time, to the special problems of the poor. And the War on Poverty brought a flood of new legislative efforts—and a flood of tax dollars—to end "being down and out" in America. One critic observing the enormous federal appropriations for studying and developing a cure for poverty observed unkindly that one way for an individual to avoid poverty was to study it. Such doubters were infrequent, though, as most Americans supported the Johnson administration program.

Myths die hard, especially political myths, and two decades after the discovery of poverty in America, the subject remains on the nation's agenda. Politicians continue to talk compassionately about the poor— still mostly at election time. Economics textbooks still devote a chapter to poverty. For all the concern, however, the distribution of income in the United States (before taxes and transfers) has remained fairly constant over the past thirty-five years. As Table 8.1 shows, before, during, and after the War on Poverty years, the top 20 percent of American income earners have continued to receive 41 to 42 percent of all income, while

Table 8.1   Shares of Earned Income by Families (in percentages), 1947–1979

Income Level	1947	1950	1956	1960	1964	1969	1975	1979
Poorest fifth	5.0	4.5	5.0	4.9	5.2	5.6	5.4	5.2
Second fifth	11.8	12.0	12.4	12.0	12.0	12.3	11.8	11.6
Third fifth	17.0	17.4	17.8	17.6	17.7	17.6	17.6	17.5
Fourth fifth	23.1	23.5	23.7	23.6	24.0	23.4	24.1	24.1
Richest fifth	43.0	42.6	41.2	42.0	41.1	41.0	41.1	41.5

Source: Roger A. Herriot and Herman P. Miller, "The Taxes We Pay," Conference Board Record, May 1971, p. 40; and U.S. Bureau of the Census, Statistical Abstract, 1980, p. 454.

the poorest 20 percent earn about 5 percent. About 14 percent of all Americans (about 32 million people) live below the government-established poverty "threshold" (annual income of about $9300 in 1982 for a family of four). Figure 8.1 gives a brief profile of who the American poor are and where they live.

Recently, there has been much rethinking of the so-called poverty question and the income redistribution efforts of the War on Poverty. In 1981, another annoying little book, George Gilder's *Wealth and Poverty*, captured large audiences by proclaiming that government should abandon its efforts at income redistribution. Gilder's book, which was distributed freely by President Reagan to White House guests, argued that all of our antipoverty efforts caused more damage than good. In fact, the poor have been harmed the most.

We have come full circle in two decades—from massive efforts to end poverty and create greater income equality, to ending these programs altogether. Which approach in the long run is best, of course, is a matter of heated debate. What isn't debatable, though, is the fact that great income disparities exist in America and that many Americans remain, as did so many in the past, poor.

SYNOPSIS. The Conservative argument holds that income inequality is natural and that efforts to change it through taxes and transfers will diminish the entire society's well-being. According to the Liberal argument, a more equalitarian distribution of income is humane and necessary. The Radical argument contends that income disparity is normal and even needed in capitalism, but at the same time undermines the capitalist system.

FIGURE 8.1   WHO THE POOR ARE*

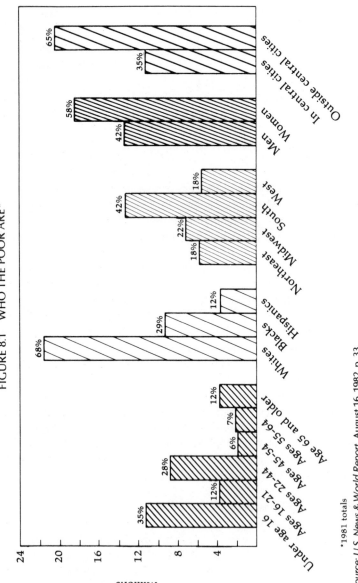

*1981 totals

Source: U.S. News & World Report, August 16, 1982, p. 33.

Anticipating the Arguments

- Why do Conservatives believe that public charitable efforts are essentially self-defeating and harmful to the poor themselves?

- On what grounds do Liberals argue that we currently are backing away from our responsibilities to the society's least fortunate?

- What are the basic philosophical differences between Conservatives and Liberals on the "ideal" distribution of income?

- How do you account for the Radicals' argument that our past income redistributional efforts have at best failed and perhaps have made the income gap widen?

The Conservative Argument

A unifying feature of all centralist (Liberal and Radical) programs for the past one hundred years has been the call for equalitarianism in income. The "Robin Hood" illusion is the very beginning of any collectivist's social dream. In the United States, income redistribution efforts appear in two general forms: (1) a highly progressive income tax structure aimed at piling the expense of social spending upon the upper-income elements of the society and (2) a vast giveaway of these appropriations to the poor and the nonproductive groups within the nation. Both schemes rest upon serious errors of economic and social thinking, which we explored in the last issue on productivity, but which deserve fuller elaboration and criticism.

A JUST SYSTEM OF REWARDS

Distribution of income should be governed by the simple and equitable principle that all members of a society should receive according to what they, or whatever they own, are able to produce. The abilities, tastes, and occupational interests of individuals vary. People value work and leisure differently. Some individuals are willing to forgo an assured lower income in favor of taking a risk and possibly earning more. Enforced equality of income utterly fails to consider these possibilities. It presumes that greater social satisfaction is attained by income parity than by letting people make their own valuations of what money means to them.

Consider, for instance, a person who is quite content to live on $100 a week. From this person's point of view, needs are satisfied and the right balance between leisure and work has been achieved. To transfer to this person one quarter of the wages of another person who makes $200 a week will hardly increase the first person's welfare or happiness. At the same time it subtracts much satisfaction from the second person, who is willing to work hard enough to earn the $200 wage. If we could now add up the relative satisfactions of the two workers, it would be lower after redistribution than before. In other words, proof is lacking that a more equal income distribution actually maximizes community satisfaction.

At another level, equalitarianism leads to more serious troubles. Enforcing equal distribution of income penalizes the industrious and inventive and subsidizes those with less initiative. If the industrious fail to obtain rewards for their talents and work, they naturally will slacken their efforts. As a result, the total product of the society is lessened. In the subsequent equalitarian redistribution, everyone gets less than before. Just how far the detrimental effects of income equalization can go in destroying a society is evident in Great Britain. There, subsidy for nonproduction and confiscation of earned income have lowered national output and put the nation at a disadvantage in world trade. The best minds and the nation's capital have fled to other countries. At home there is a shabby equality and mediocrity.

While the discussion so far has been mostly with regard to individual labor, it also applies to individuals' command over capital and wealth. Appropriating the wealth of one to support another denies the individual's right to property and will lead to inefficiency and economic contraction in the whole society. (Whether the wealth is inherited or has been earned by the individual is irrelevant.) This is not just an economic matter. Seizures of wages and property are violations of freedom. It is not a big step from telling people what their income will be to telling them what work to do or what ideas to think.

Of course we must move from the realm of abstract theory justifying income inequality and protecting property rights, into the real world. There, taxes must be collected to carry on the business of government (even if that business is excessive). And, to help those who are not able to take care of themselves, transfer payments are necessary. However, taxes and transfers must express the principles just summarized.

TOWARD A FAIR TAX STRUCTURE

The federal tax system, which collects more than two thirds of all our taxes, is characterized by three serious errors: (1) the graduated personal income tax, (2) fear of concentrated inherited wealth, and (3) the belief that taxing corporations is somehow "painless" to individuals.

Income Taxes   Philosophically, the progressive personal income tax is a discriminatory confiscation of some people's property and a limiting of their rights and freedom. Economically, however, it makes even less sense. If successively higher tax rates are to be applied to increases in income, then working to acquire more income provides less real reward. The diminished reward reduces the desire to work and, as we saw in our study of the productivity problem, also reduces the entire society's savings, investments, and growth rate. Moreover, as Arthur Laffer and others have pointed out, the higher tax rates yield less and less receipts as they discourage additional earnings. Thus, the progressive income tax approach, apart from its unfairness and adverse economic effects, is also self-deflating.

Some of course, will not accept these arguments; but there is other evidence of folly in our progressive tax structure. Rather than having the intended "Robin Hood" effect, it has encouraged legal tax evasion by creating numerous tax loopholes: tax-free status for state and municipal bonds, capital gains privileges, unfair "effective" rates (lower for single taxpayers), expense accounts, and so on. Thus, for many taxpayers the actual rates are much lower than the published rates on their incomes. Since not everyone enjoys the same loophole privileges, tax collection is uneven and unfair. Make no mistake, true

Conservatives are not heartened to learn that several hundred million-aires legally avoid tax payments every year. Quite apart from these in-equities, our tax structure encourages individuals to take actions that may save taxes but are economically foolish. They may decide to buy tax-free municipal bonds rather than corporate bonds. Thus, urban debt is traded off against corporate expansion.

Inheritance Taxes   Closely associated with the assault on high-in-come earners is the attack on inherited wealth. Some Liberals have proposed a virtually confiscatory inheritance tax. Again, this must be opposed on philosophical principle and on the grounds that it will dis-courage work and savings incentives. However, another point should be made. The irrational fear among Liberals (and Radicals) of concen-trations of private wealth fails to recognize that wealth and its associ-ated power is less concentrated today than in the past. Most of the great nineteenth-century family holdings—Gould, Carnegie, Astor, and the like—exist only in the history books as philanthropy and off-spring deficient in entrepreneurial acuity have dissipated the inheri-tance. Even in the cases where the old family names remain in the news—the Rockefellers, the DuPonts, and the Mellons, for instance—the family fortunes have been divided and redivided among heirs to the point where no single scion has much real financial power. While the ability to acquire and pass on wealth remains an important factor in encouraging work and saving, untaxed inheritances are scarcely an invitation for a plutocratic class to seize power.

Corporate Taxes   The political custom of hitting corporations with high taxes goes back to the days of Franklin Roosevelt. After all, cor-porations don't vote, so higher corporate profits taxes are politically painless. This is very shortsighted. There is no such thing as a painless tax.

In the issue on productivity we noted the effect of corporate taxes in reducing a firm's investment funds, and there is no need to present that argument again. However, apart from the effect of corporate taxes in lowering American productivity and overall economic per-formance, there are a number of undesirable income redistribution ef-fects. First, a tax on a corporation's profits is really a tax on the own-er's earnings. Thus, those receiving dividends get taxed twice—first with a corporate profits tax and then with a personal income tax on dividend income. Second, it is possible that some corporations are able to pass on some of their tax burdens to customers in the form of higher prices. If this is done, then consumers—very often poor consumers—end up paying the "painless" corporate profits tax.

The only intelligent solution is a simple, no-loophole, proportional income tax. This "flat rate tax" without deductions and exemptions probably would lower taxes for most taxpayers. (Some economists have estimated that a rate as low as 18 percent on all personal income would be sufficient.) Such a system would be fair in that those who pay more would do so in proportion to their income and the benefits they receive from government. It would be democratic in that special interests could not have their way with Congress or the Internal Revenue Service.

THE WELFARE PROGRAM

While taxes are one way of equalizing income, a second and more disruptive method for doing so is the welfare system. Broadly speaking, welfare includes a wide variety of subsidies paid to individuals to offset low incomes. These include direct support transfers (as in the Aid to Families with Dependent Children program), public housing, minimum-wage laws, unemployment insurance, Medicaid, and Social Security.

Table 8.2 illustrates the present extent of federal social spending to provide a so-called "safety net" for Americans, as well as the fantastic growth of this net over the past decade. Looking at the data somewhat differently, the American welfare system equals about 18 percent of the nation's gross national product (GNP). More astounding than these aggregates, though, is the marginal growth in welfare spending. In still depressionary 1940, it accounted for just 6 percent, and in 1965, during the "giveaway" years of President Johnson's War on Poverty, it amounted to only 14 percent of the GNP. The rate of growth in welfare programs and spending is particularly dangerous since it means that ever-greater tax sacrifices must be demanded of working citizens. For many workers, after-tax income is less than welfare grants paid to nonworkers.

Apart from their cost, however, have the welfare programs and other efforts to assist low-income Americans attained their goals?

Whatever their intentions, most of these programs fail to do what they promise. Indeed, they often do more harm than good. Aid to Families with Dependent Children (AFDC), given only to mothers and

Table 8.2   The Growth of Social Benefits (in billions of dollars), 1970-1981

	1970	1981	% Change
Social Security	26.3	119.4	354
Social Security disability	2.8	16.9	504
Medicare	6.7	38.7	478
Civil service pensions	2.7	17.3	541
Military pensions	2.8	13.6	386
Railroad pensions	1.6	5.2	225
Unemployment compensation	3.0	24.3	710
Veterans benefits	6.9	15.5	125
Medicaid	2.7	16.4	507
Food stamps and nutrition	1.0	13.4	1240
Aid for Families with Dependent Children	4.1	7.7	88
Supplementary income	—	6.5	—
Housing subsidies	.8	6.6	725

Source: Economic Report of the President, 1982.

children in the absence of a working father, has broken up families. Public housing programs, which involve tearing down old neighborhoods and building new housing complexes, actually have caused a shortage of low-income rentals and forced rents upward. Minimum-wage laws, rather than assuring a desired wage, have destroyed marginal jobs. Unemployment insurance induces people not to work. Medicaid has forced health costs upward. Virtually all cash-granting welfare programs encourage fraud, and as a result our welfare system is not only excessively expensive, but it acts to encourage criminality. The list of tragedies resulting from well-intended social tinkering is endless. On top of all that, we are burdened with a vast bureaucracy at all levels of government to administer these programs.

Beyond their more obvious defects, welfare efforts are particularly lamentable because they create a strong disincentive to work and discourage people from improving themselves. People have to be poor in order to qualify for welfare protection, and they have to stay poor to keep getting it. Thus, our welfare system has created a vast and permanent subculture of the disadvantaged. Meanwhile, the rest of the society must pay support costs.

The ideal solution would be to end such a system of transfers, but realistically we must face the fact that some people are indeed unable to care for themselves or will be the victims of lags and "stickiness" in the economy. We shall have to pay some welfare support. That support, however, should not reduce the incentives to work or for self-improvement, and it should be administered as simply as possible.

As with proportional, no-exemptions income tax, welfare payments should follow simple and unalterable rules. First, we should determine a minimum subsistence level of income for a family, and assure it through a negative income tax payment. Additional private income may be added to this figure until the direct payment plus the private earnings raise total income to levels of legal taxability. At this point, the recipient becomes just another taxpayer. These transfer arrangements, however, should be tied to a "workfare" system for all able-bodied recipients. The obligation to be ready and willing to accept work is a fair one. At a minimum, this probably would require registration at employment offices and active job searching. Obviously there are a number of possible ways to set up a negative income tax program, but Conservatives should support those that encourage work incentives, lead to dismantling most present subsidy efforts, demand the least administrative overhead, and are subject to rules and not discretion.

The Conservative, while recognizing the adverse effects of taxes and transfers, also understands the need for them. However, taxing and transferring efforts must be based on economic reason and not the collectivist obsession with creating greater income equality. The market distributes income. When politicians do, economic order is lost.

The Liberal Argument

As Conservatives have correctly pointed out, the tax and transfer efforts to close the income gap in the United States largely have failed; however, the failure is not a matter of having created the "collectivist" income equality that Conservatives oppose. The problem is that taxes and welfare have not reversed the chronic tendency toward income inequality. While there has not been much change in the shares of total income going to different proportions of the population, the dollar gap between the bottom and the top has been increasing. This is not the result of the market recognizing hard work and rewarding it (as the Conservatives argue). Rather, it reflects a fundamental inequality of opportunity.

This inequality has left America with a vast subculture of poverty. The dimensions and distribution of this poverty may be seen in the following data:

1. More than 14 percent of the total population lives in poverty.
2. Black poverty is four times greater than white poverty, with more than 30 percent of all nonwhites living in poverty.
3. Poverty hits the old and the young very hard: About a fifth of those over sixty-five live in poverty, and about 40 percent of all those classified as poor are under the age of eighteen.
4. Poverty affects working Americans: More than two-fifths of those classed as poor come from households in which the head was reported as employed during part of the year, a fourth from families whose head worked the entire year.
5. Poverty and poor education are closely related, with more than half of all the poor reporting less than nine years of education.
6. Families headed by women have a high incidence of poverty: About one third of all female-headed families are poor, and, at the same time, female-head-of-household poverty describes more than a third of all the poor.
7. Poverty is self-perpetuating: The highest correlation between poverty and any other attribute is that the poor themselves come from poverty-stricken backgrounds.

THE ADVANTAGE OF EQUALITY

Poverty, then, is the result of inadequate education, poor health, racism, sexism, and a lagging economy. Individuals do not surmount these obstacles through their own personalities. Poverty, of course, breeds more poverty, just as wealth takes care of its own. To believe that the existing shares of income reflect people's ability is naive. To fail to see that income disparity is the root of social decay and political instability is simple blindness. At bottom, the question of more equitable distribution of income will not stand or fall on such microeconomic questions as, "Is total happiness maximized?" A more equal (although certainly not perfectly equal) distribution is needed for humane purposes and to hold society together.

In terms of a macroeconomic analysis of the problem, modern economic theory shows us that a more equal distribution of income tends to improve general economic conditions. With income spread among larger numbers of people, a nation's propensity to consume will rise. This increase in total demand for goods creates jobs and stimulates economic expansion. On the other hand, income inequality leads to excessive savings and a slowdown in economic activity. The exaggerated Conservative concern for protecting work incentives through reduced taxes and maintaining income disparities has exactly the opposite effect: It abolishes jobs.

DEFENDING PROGRESSIVE TAXATION

Ever since the adoption of the progressive income tax in 1912, the United States has been committed to the principle of a more equal distribution of real income. The goal is not a perfectly equal distribution, since that would affect work and saving incentives. Liberals have never encouraged confiscatory taxes on upper incomes. They do believe that, in recognition of the ability to pay and real benefits received, the well-to-do should pay proportionately more as their income rises. The tax system in practice has been another matter.

The progressive intent of our federal income tax structure has been offset by loopholes that permit wholesale legal tax evasion. Almost all the beneficiaries of these loopholes are businesses and wealthy individuals. As Conservatives correctly point out, the tax laws permit the well-to-do to pay lower effective rates than the middle and lower classes. At the state and local level, regressive taxation is common. These units of government rely heavily on sales taxes and property taxes, which fall proportionately more heavily on those with lower incomes. In sum, the existing tax structure fails to reach those individual and corporate tax bases able to pay more, and puts the burden on people in the middle and at the bottom of the income scale. In many cases our taxes actually cause greater real income inequality.

Liberals want thorough tax reform to restore the principle of progressive taxation. Special loopholes for the privileged should be closed. Liberals do not advocate taxation without discretionary exemptions, however. Taxing is integral to fiscal policy, and tax incentives may be needed from time to time to encourage or discourage certain spending decisions by business and individuals. For instance, limited exemptions or deductions to home builders can be used to stimulate the construction industry in times of economic contraction. The no-discretion approach of most Conservatives is too arbitrary and limits flexibility in fiscal policy. Whatever discretionary changes are made, however, the principle of progressive taxation should be sustained.

STOPPING THE ASSAULT ON WELFARE

Probably the most enduring Conservative misinformation about the dimensions and cost of our welfare system stems from their assumption that most social spending goes only to the undeserving poor. In fact, only about one sixth of all so-called social spending (less than one twelfth of the federal budget) is allocated specifically to the needy.

As Table 8.3 indicates, the nonpoor are the chief recipients of federal transfer payments. Even if the Conservatives succeeded in completely sacrificing the truly poor to the requirements of maintaining work incentives for the well-to-do, it hardly would make a dent in federal spending and the federal tax bill. Ultimately, their budgetary ad-

Table 8.3 Social Programs in Federal Budget and Shares of Total Budget by Eligibility, 1980 Fiscal Year

Eligibility Not Determined By Need: 36.2%
  Military pensions
  Civil service pensions
  Social Security
  Medicare
  Unemployment Insurance

Eligibility Partially Determined by Need: 4.4%
  Veterans pensions
  Veterans health benefits
  School Lunch and other health programs

Eligibility Determined by Need: 8.5%
  Medicaid
  Student aid
  Rent subsidies
  Food Stamps
  Supplemental Security Income
  Aid for Families with Dependent Children

Source: Peter G. Petersen, "No More Free Lunch for the Middle Class," *New York Times Magazine*, January 17, 1982, p. 41

versary is not the poor but middle-income Americans. As the old comic-strip character Pogo once observed, "We have found the enemy and it is us." The truly needy are only a scapegoat for Conservative attacks. A serious budgetary reduction in the area of social outlays would pull the safety net from under the poor today, but tomorrow it would pull the rug from under almost everyone else who is nonrich. When this fact is understood, it should be evident to all Americans that either the Conservative case against social spending is empty rhetoric or it is a challenge to be opposed by practically everyone.

The recent attack upon the principle of maintaining minimum levels of social welfare has not been limited merely to questioning the level of public spending. The long and bitter struggle to create a single federally administered welfare system, which has proceeded ever so slowly since the New Deal era, was challenged directly in 1982 by President Reagan. Under his "New Federalism" plan, the president urged the gradual return of social welfare budgets to the individual states. Each state in its own wisdom eventually would decide what its poor would need to survive. Never mind that this would return us to the old "local" welfare system of Herbert Hoover's time and that it would dismantle fifty years of efforts to create a national program; the "New Federalism" fits perfectly into the Conservative's antigovernment scheme of things.

The "New Federalism" has some obvious economic shortcomings. First, the overall costs to state governments, already hampered by a lack of tax base, is estimated by AFL-CIO economists to rise as high as $86 billion per year by 1991. Although some Federal monies would be available initially, virtually the entire welfare bill would be shifted to the states as the years pass. Second, the nation's welfare burdens and its ability to carry these burdens is not distributed equitably among the individual states. Some, such as Michigan, have a heavy responsibility but dwindling capacity to pay, while others, like Georgia, have a smaller burden and a greater carrying capacity.

Aside from the fact that the "New Federalism" is a dangerous and questionable exercise in creative accounting—making federal spending appear to decline by shifting it to the individual states—it certainly will worsen the problems of the poor. Inequities certainly will grow as each state arbitrarily establishes its "social minimum." In the 1930s, some states denied voting rights to those on public assistance. In the 1950s, "welfare" in some Mississippi townships consisted of $75 and a one-way bus ticket to Detroit. Even in the "socially concerned" 1970s, Mississippi's AFDC (Aid for Families with Dependent Children) payments, which are based on a formula of federal-state-local sharing of costs, paid benefits only one tenth those paid in Massachusetts.

THE NEED FOR A NATIONAL WELFARE SYSTEM

The first step in improving the welfare system is to place it totally under federal jurisdiction. A nationwide minimum must be established and must be paid for federally, not locally, so as to equalize the cost burden.

There has been much talk in recent years about a federally guaranteed annual income (GAI) or negative income tax (NIT). These methods of providing a national social minimum deserve policy attention, and even Conservatives like Milton Friedman have advanced some support for the idea. However, the basic problem with GAI and NIT proposals is how to determine and administer a minimum that helps only the genuinely poor and does not at the same time destroy work incentives. While the GAI or NIT problem may be resolved and one of these cash payment solutions may be adopted in the future, the federalizing and redesigning of existing programs is a more plausible current solution.

Let us assume that the nation adopted a minimum guarantee of two-thirds of the poverty level income for the 32 million Americans who live below it and that the federal government took over the present state and local welfare contributions up to that level. Such a proposal has been studied by the Committee for Economic Development, a prestigious policy group of business leaders. Applying their estimates of additional costs to the present situation would amount to about a 5 percent increase in the federal budget. While not modest, this would be a small outlay in a federal budget of over $500 billion. Moreover, such a guaranteed income approach would reduce the need for the present multiplicity of federal programs and effect savings by shrinking the overblown federal welfare bureaucracy. It also would reduce state and municipal welfare costs, although local government units of course would be free to add to their welfare minimum if they saw fit.

While reasonable minimum welfare payments are necessary (and should be higher than those now administered under our present patchwork programs), welfare is not the real solution to eliminating poverty or income inequality. Welfare programs designed merely to pacify the poor create a permanent poor. A useful federal program aimed at greater income equalization must attack the roots of the problem. This means that welfare efforts must be related to educational and job-creating programs. Racism and sexism must be attacked directly by law. Welfare efforts should encourage work and stimulate jobs. However, they should rely on the carrot, not the stick. The Conservatives' plan for virtually starving people into work, coupled as it is with their belief in the merit of income inequality, is a return to an earlier, barbaric capitalism.

Of course, the capacity of any society simultaneously to end poverty and ameliorate income disparities depends on its own economic vitality. Regardless of efforts to improve our taxing and welfare systems, little can be done unless the economy is expanding.

The Radical Argument

Although they may appear miles apart on the question of income distribution policy, Conservatives and Liberals share a common perspective: Poverty is poor people's fault. To the Conservative, low incomes or no earned income at all reflect the market-determined value of an individual's talents and initiative. Defects of character and skill of the poor themselves are the roots of their poverty. To the Liberal, poverty is also the result of a person's circumstances—race, sex, insufficient education, or some other characteristic of the individual. Conservatives, of course, are content to let the poor struggle out of their condition by themselves, while Liberals are quick to apply moderately redistributive tax and transfer programs and other social policy band-aids for the economically "disadvantaged." By looking only at the characteristics of the poor, albeit in different ways, neither Conservatives nor Liberals recognize that poverty is the system's fault; that extreme income inequality, with its attendant suffering is essential to the capitalist order.

THE DUAL LABOR MARKET AND ENDURING POVERTY

Contrary to general impressions, very few of America's poor are poor because they don't work. At least two thirds of the families with income below the poverty line have one or more members working at a job of some sort.

In a capitalist society, work is the primary determinant of income. The work you do and what you are paid for your work set absolute limits upon your participation in the American Dream. Skipping for a minute the situation of the very few, who through inherited wealth and privileged position need not work at all, the rest of us are required to work or to accept the handouts of those who do. Yet, those of us who work do not face the same equal opportunity.

Clearly, two different and discernible sectors exist in American labor markets. In one, which we might call the *primary* sector and which is familiar to most persons reading these pages, work involves reasonable wages, fairly pleasant working conditions, job security and stability, recognition for industriousness and initiative, and a real chance for improving one's economic lot. This is not to say the work is always stimulating, but it is at least dependable and monetarily rewarding enough to build a reasonably secure and stable life. It includes the world of the white-collar manager and professional as well as the upper end of the blue-collar elements of the society. The primary sector is the work world of what commonly is called "middle-class America."

The *secondary* sector of our labor markets, although everywhere visible and constantly growing, hardly receives our attention. There, jobs are less attractive. They pay less (never much more than minimum wage) and have little security. Working conditions are poor, and experience teaches workers that there is little likelihood of promotion or upward movement, however hard they work. Work itself is usually only occasional, with frequent lengthy periods of unemployment. The secondary sector is the work world of the poor. It is the sweatshop, the fast-food restaurant, or the discount retail outlet.

The obvious Conservative response at this point might be, "Leave the secondary labor market for the primary market if you don't like it!" Such advice utterly fails to recognize these facts about secondary labor: (1) the secondary labor market, unstable as it is for individuals, is a source of considerable profit to entrepreneurs; (2) the secondary labor market is growing much faster than the primary market; and (3) the scarring effects of being caught within the secondary market make upward movement virtually impossible. In other words, a segment of the population caught in the chronic poverty of secondary labor markets cannot break out because their low-paid labor is profitable, because opportunities of entrance into better-paid positions are limited by the production-for-profit system, and because the poor are, in a sense, trained to be poor.

The self-sustaining nature of secondary labor markets is helped along by the fact that its members are easily identifiable. They are black, Hispanic, female, young, or possess some other characteristic usually identified by employers with "marginal" labor. Thus stereotyped, few are ever able to obtain an equal opportunity with primary-market workers in vying for primary-sector employment. A self-perpetuating discrimination tends ever to hold them back.

At this point the Liberal usually appears, arguing that education and enforcement of "equal opportunity" laws will break the poverty cycle. However, the facts simply don't support such a conclusion. In the early 1980s, black Americans continue to earn only about 60 percent of white income—about the same as two decades ago, before the passage of extensive antidiscrimination legislation. Meanwhile black unemployment continues to be twice as high as the national average. For women the evidence is pretty much the same; in fact, women's earnings actually have declined as a percentage of men's income since the 1950s (to 56 percent). To be sure, at the very top, among the few women and blacks who attained higher educational levels, the black–white and female–male income gaps have closed somewhat. However, rather than proving that education will raise earnings, as Liberals claim, this more accurately reflects the "tokenism" of the past two decades—a little space at the top to placate civil rights and women's movement advocates.

TAXES AND WELFARE TRANSFERS FROM THE NONRICH TO THE RICH

In terms of understanding the role of taxes and welfare in capitalist society, both Conservatives and Liberals are correct on two different points. First, as Conservatives argue, the combined income effects of our tax and transfer policies must not destroy work incentives. Second, as Liberals argue, tax and welfare policies also are intended to ameliorate the most glaring inequalities in income, or at least hide them. In American capitalism, maldistribution of income is essential to support the work ethic, but too big a gap erodes the credibility of American political and economic institutions. Thus, taxes and transfers walk a tightrope, maintaining yet hiding the income gap.

Our national tax system does not close the income gap but, in fact, tends to widen it. While the well-known tax loopholes of the rich allow legal evasion, we tend to forget the heavily regressive effect of certain taxes on the poor and the middle class.

Take property taxes for instances. These account for about two thirds of collections by local governments. A Senate study in 1973 determined that property taxes, whether paid by individual homeowners or by tenants in their monthly rents, averaged about 4.9 percent of family income. However, the rate was 16.9 percent for those earning less than $2,000. For those earning over $25,000, the rate was a mere 2.9 percent.

Sales taxes, the other important source of state and local revenue, are also regressive. As these taxes have been extended to cover necessities, they fall more and more heavily on those with little discretionary income. Obviously the taxes on a wealthy person's electricity are much less of a burden than are electricity taxes for a low-income worker, regardless of the number of rooms in the wealthy person's estate.

The result in absolute terms is that lower-income and middle-income groups pay for most city and state governmental expenditures. They receive fewer of the social benefits. The poor have less police and fire protection, poorer roads and schools, and inadequate sanitation services. Thus, a serious effort to develop a fair—let alone progressive—income redistribution must start at the level of local tax inequality.

At the federal level, although politicians constantly promise to close the loopholes that benefit the rich, they are unlikely to do so. For one thing, loopholes are the result of political power and lobbying—something that is not likely to end very soon. Not only that, but many are seen as economically necessary. For instance, the mortgage and property tax credits of middle- and upper-income taxpayers serve as a stimulus to the construction industry. Business investment tax credits are intended to encourage business expansion. Therefore, the discretionary use of tax policies for fiscal manipulation or to keep interest groups happy will always create loopholes that benefit the few greatly and the masses slightly.

Equalization of income through taxation cannot be a serious objective in a capitalist system so long as the powerful control government. Under capitalism the tax structure will remain merely another device to transfer income and wealth ("surplus" in Marxist terms) from the nonrich to the rich.

Meanwhile, the primary function of welfare measures is not humanitarianism but legitimation. The problems of the poor are always a social threat. This has been especially obvious in the recent history of black Americans. Although the deteriorating condition of the ghettos was well known before the urban riots of 1964 and 1965, there was no expansion of welfare programs or benefits. Only in the wake of the riots were AFDC payments tripled and other welfare programs enlarged. Life did not improve as a result of this welfarism, but, by the early 1970s, the combination of massive police armament, drugs, and internal political change had brought a calm to the ghetto. Precisely at this time, President Nixon initiated his "benign neglect" policy of closing down the urban welfare apparatus. The pretext was the need for governmental economy; the basic reason was that such legitimation transfers were no longer politically essential.

The welfare system is as much an economic benefit to the well-to-do as it is to the needy. Welfare dollars buy the goods of corporate America. They assure doctors, dentists, and drug companies of payment (usually excessive) for health services. Poor people, in fact, get a very small amount of the public dole. In 1981, federal spending for the truly needy (where income eligibility tests are required) amounted to only 8.5 percent of the federal budget (see Table 8.3). Exactly how vulnerable the truly needy are and how weak our commitment to maintaining social welfare is has become obvious in the Reagan years, when ruthless budget cutting has increased the agony of the poor. However, while the poor's safety net was being removed, business tax cuts, an enlarged military budget (taking almost half of federal expenditures), and a variety of corporate subsidies provided a comfortable cushion for the undeserving. The Revenue Reform Bill of 1981, for instance, provided deductions and exemptions to individuals (practically all of whom were in the top 20-percent income bracket) worth $173 billion. Investors, business owners, and corporations got another $100 billion in special tax reductions. There is little concern that the recipients of these "corporate welfare" transfers might be losing their incentive because of "living off the dole." As someone aptly observed, "In America, we have free enterprise for the poor and welfare for the wealthy."

A RADICAL PROGRAM TO END INEQUALITY

It is obvious that the combined effect of our tax and transfer system is to maintain income inequality. It serves the system well. The welfare poor act as a potential labor pool to be tapped as needed and to be used as a check on excessive labor demands by those who work.

With large numbers of people held in a "poverty reserve," unions cannot push too strongly against capital's power. Inequality also serves the purpose of disciplining labor. Maintaining the bottom layers of society at bare subsistence levels does provide a work "incentive." Given the oppressive and alienating nature of most work in America, wages and the hope for better wages are practically the only device to keep labor in the market and keep it producing. Inequality also serves an important social purpose of dividing the working class. The overtaxed and underpaid worker frequently turns against the welfare-supported nonworker. Nonworkers often hate themselves and those above them who have comparatively slight income advantages. The source of income inequality is thus ignored.

From a Radical view, income equalization is crucial. In terms of short-run socialist reforms, this must mean a total renovation of the tax structure—elimination of taxes on incomes below a certain level, along with the guarantee of a *reasonable* minimum income for everyone, working or not. The elimination of tax loopholes, adoption of high and steeply progressive taxes on all income, and virtually confiscatory taxes on accumulated wealth would be essential. At the same time, the extent and content of social welfare programs should be altered to fit human needs.

All of these steps, even though they fall short of actual long-run social ownership of capital, would be unacceptable to defenders of the capitalist system. However, the system's failure, indeed its inability, to achieve some measure of income equalization—along with the chronic problems of unemployment, inflation, and fiscal crisis—erode popular acceptance of existing inequities. Thus it is likely that general pressure for tax reform and more humane welfare programs will grow. The realization that inequality in income and wealth is not legitimate very probably will signal the beginning of the end of the production-for-profit system. At any rate, it is in the area of income inequality that the contradictions of modern American capitalism are most obvious.

PART 3

CONCLUSION

Final Thoughts and Suggested Readings

Having reached the end of this volume of debates on contemporary economic issues, it is probable that the reader expects (perhaps even hopes for) the author to make his own pitch—to say straight out which of the representative paradigms is correct and which is not, perhaps to unveil his own grand program. Indeed, the opportunity is tempting. For an economist, it is practically a reflex to try to get in the last word, especially his own last word. However, after much thought, I decided that such a conclusion would spoil the entire effort. The book was undertaken to present the differing ideological alternatives as objectively as space and writing talents allowed so that the reader would be free to make her or his own hard choices on matters of economic policy.

I can hear some readers complaining: "Cop-out! You're avoiding presenting your own preferences and your own conclusions. You've taken the easy way out of the swamp." No so. Delivering my own final polemic would in truth be ever so easy. But the book has been about questions and choices. The reader, then, shall be left in the uncomfortable position of making his or her own choice among the paradigms and policy questions surveyed here. And that is the way it should be.

This perspective, however, must not be misunderstood. The author has not intended to produce a "relativistic" conclusion in which any choice will do and one choice is as good as any other. The point is for the reader to make a *good* choice, and some policy choices *are* better than others. However, only a reasoned analysis of the facts and a critical study of the "truths" of this world will permit any of us to make wise choices.

The British economist Joan Robinson has said it best:

> Social life will always present mankind with a choice of evils. No metaphysical solution that can ever be formulated will seem satisfactory for long. The solutions offered by economists were no less delusory than those of the theologians that they displaced.
>
> All the same we must not abandon the hope that economics can make an advance towards science, or the faith that enlightenment is not useless. It is necessary to clear the decaying remnants of obsolete metaphysics out of the way before we can go forward.
>
> The first essential for economists, arguing amongst themselves, is to "try very seriously," as Professor Popper says that natural scientists do, "to avoid talking at cross purposes."*

Before we can "avoid talking at cross purposes" on economic matters, we must understand our fundamental differences in opinion and interpretation. Hopefully, this book has identified some of these important differences for the reader.

In undertaking this task, any author would be sorely tested. While trying to submerge personal biases, one also must master the biases of others. Perhaps I have not entirely succeeded on either count. Only the reader can judge. Nevertheless, such an undertaking is extremely educational. It compels one to work through unfamiliar logic and ideas and weigh them against one's own beliefs. For readers who desire to dig deeper into economic ideologies and their application to contemporary issues, the following bibliography offers some landmark readings in the respective Conservative, Liberal, and Radical schools of economic thought.

---

*Joan Robinson, *Economic Philosophy* (Garden City, N.Y.: Anchor Books, 1964), pp. 147–148.

Conservative

Banfield, Edward C. *The Unheavenly City*. Boston: Little, Brown, and Co., 1970.

Buckley, William. *Up from Liberalism*. New York: Honor Books, 1959.

Friedman, Milton. *Capitalism and Freedom*. Chicago: University of Chicago Press, 1962.

_____. *Free to Choose*. New York: Harcourt Brace Jovanovich, 1980.

Gilder, George. *Wealth and Power*. New York: Basic Books, 1981.

Hazlitt, Henry. *The Failure of the "New Economics": An Analysis of the Keynesian Fallacies*. Princeton, N.J.: Van Nostrand Co., 1959.

Kirk, Russell. *The Conservative Mind*. Chicago: H. Regnery & Co., 1954.

Knight, Frank. *Freedom and Reform*. New York: Harper & Row, 1947.

Rand, Ayn. *Capitalism: The Unknown Ideal*. New York: New American Library, Signet Books, 1967.

Simon, William E. *A Time for Action*. New York: Berkley Books, 1980.

Simons, Henry C. *A Positive Program for Laissez-Faire*. Chicago: University of Chicago Press, 1934.

Smith, Adam. *An Inquiry into the Nature and Causes of the Wealth of Nations*, 1776.

Von Hayek, Friedrich. *The Road to Serfdom*. Chicago: University of Chicago Press, 1944.

Von Mises, Ludwig. *Socialism: An Economic and Sociological Analysis*. New Haven, Conn.: Yale University Press, 1959.

Liberal

Berle, Adolf A. *The Twentieth Century Capitalist Revolution*. New York: Harcourt Brace Jovanovich, 1954.

Clark, John M. *Alternative to Serfdom*. New York: Vintage Books. 1960.

_____. *Social Control of Business*. New York: McGraw-Hill, 1939.

Galbraith, John Kenneth. *The Affluent Society*. Boston: Houghton Mifflin Co., 1971.

_____. *Economics and the Public Purpose*. Boston. Houghton Mifflin Co., 1973.

_____. *The New Industrial State*. Boston: Houghton Mifflin Co., 1967.

Hansen, Alvin. *The American Economy*. New York: McGraw-Hill, 1957.

Heilbroner, Robert. "The Future of Capitalism," in *The Limits of American Capitalism*. New York: Harper & Row, 1966.

Heller, Walter W. *The Economy: Old Myths and New Realities*. New York: W. W. Norton & Co., 1976.

Keynes, John M. *The General Theory of Employment, Interest, and Money.* New York: Harcourt Brace, 1936.

Lekachman, Robert. *The Age of Keynes.* New York: Random House, 1966.

Okun, Arthur M. *The Political Economy of Prosperity.* New York: W. W. Norton & Co., 1970.

Reagan, Michael D. *The Managed Economy.* New York: Oxford University Press, 1963.

Shonfield, Andres. *Modern Capitalism: The Changing Balance of Public and Private Power.* New York: Oxford University Press, 1965.

Thurow, Lester C. *The Zero-Sum Society.* New York: Basic Books, 1980.

Radical

Baran, Paul. *The Political Economy of Growth.* New York: Monthly Review Press, 1957.

_____, and Paul M. Sweezy. *Monopoly Capital.* New York: Monthly Review Press, 1966.

Domhoff, William. *Who Rules America?* Englewood Cliffs, N.J.: Prentice-Hall, 1967.

Dowd, Douglas. *The Twisted Dream.* Cambridge, Mass.: Winthrop Books, 1974.

Franklin, Raymond S. *American Capitalism—Two Visions.* New York: Random House, 1977.

Kolko, Gabriel. *Wealth and Power in America.* New York: Praeger, 1962.

Magdoff, Harry. *The Age of Imperialism.* New York: Monthly Review Press, 1967.

Mandel, Ernest. *Marxist Economic Theory.* New York: Monthly Review Press, 1967.

Marx, Karl. *Capital.* 1867.

O'Connor, James. *The Fiscal Crisis of the State.* New York: St. Martin's Press, 1973.

Robinson, Joan. *An Essay on Marxian Economics.* London: Macmillan, 1942.

Sherman, Howard. *Radical Political Economy.* New York: Basic Books, 1972.

_____. *Stagflation, A Radical Theory of Unemployment and Inflation.* New York: Harper & Row, 1976.

Strachey, John. *The Nature of Capitalist Crisis.* New York: Covici, Friede, 1933.

_____. *The Theory and Practice of Socialism.* New York: Random House, 1936.

Sweezy, Paul. *The Theory of Capitalist Development.* New York: Monthly Review Press, 1942.

Williams, William A. *The Great Evasion.* Chicago: Quadrangle Books, 1964.

Index